The Resurrection of Jesus of Nazareth

WILLI MARXSEN

The Resurrection of Jesus of Nazareth

FORTRESS PRESS
Philadelphia

Translated by Margaret Kohl from the German
Die Auferstehung Jesu von Nazareth
(Gütersloher Verlagshaus Gerd Mohn, 1968)

3.25 4/09. Pub 12-22-72 (B.B.)

Library of Congress Catalog Card Number 76–120083
ISBN 0–8006–0001–0
© SCM Press Ltd 1970
First American Edition published by Fortress Press
Philadelphia 1970
Second printing 1971   **1447**
Printed in Great Britain

Contents

Preface

In the winter semester of 1967/68 I gave a series of lectures in the main lecture-hall of Münster University to members of all faculties on 'The Resurrection of Jesus of Nazareth'. I was afterwards repeatedly asked to publish the text; and I must admit that this had always been my intention. My pamphlet *Die Auferstehung Jesu als historisches und als theologisches Problem* (Gütersloh, 1964) had started a violent discussion, opinion ranging from enthusiastic agreement to passionate rejection. The views I expressed in the pamphlet played no small part in producing the third (or fourth?) application to the governing body of the Evangelical Church of Westphalia to remove me from its examining commission on the grounds of heresy. The movers of this proposal had apparently failed to notice that in the preface to the pamphlet in question I expressly stated that my intention was to offer material for discussion. There was no attempt either to discuss my thesis or to refute it on rational grounds. It was thought sufficient to establish that some of my statements were contrary to the creed. This may be true, as far as the formulation goes. But who can repeat the old formulations today without interpreting them?

My pamphlet was primarily intended for theologians. Much of it, however, has since been carried into the churches. In the process sentences have usually been torn out of their context and the context itself has been ignored; and these sentences have then been used against me. Attempts were made to stir up the churches against me with talk of their 'custodianship'. No mention was made of the fact that although according to the Reformed view the churches are the guardians of the proclamation (which is what the credal writings mean by the word 'doctrine'), they are not the guardians of theology; the fact that there is a distinction here was studiously suppressed.

It now seemed to me that material intended for theologians could also be presented in terms comprehensible to the churches in general. So I decided to leave the ghetto of a purely theological audience and to explain my views to a wider circle, taking advantage of the opportunity offered to a university teacher by the institution of the open lecture. It was not my intention to introduce a polemical note here. I simply wanted to try to present the problem as simply as possible, being convinced that the facts, soberly argued, would speak for themselves and would convince my listeners, even if they had come to the lectures armed with another view or picture. For that reason I did not want to introduce my listeners to all the discussions on the subject, still less did I propose to enlist the vast literature on the question. I meant to call hypotheses hypotheses and to explain why I entertained some of them (because without hypotheses one cannot manage at certain points). In other cases I meant to say why I simply did not know the answer. My concern was to keep the whole question outside the realm of controversy as far as possible, because controversy so often leads to blindness. I therefore stressed in the opening lecture that no one need expect anything sensational, but that I was inviting my hearers to think through and examine my arguments for themselves.

In the end I did not quite attain my purpose, because of the 'current events' that took place during the period of the lectures. I felt bound to take notice of these because most of my hearers were aware of them and had the right to expect me to state my position. I neither could nor would disregard the fact that I was lecturing in Münster, Westphalia, in the winter semester of 1967/68. These 'current events' consisted of two declarations. (I am not calling them current events simply because they belonged to that particular period but because I am pretty certain that they will remain merely current, in the sense of ephemeral.) The first declaration was issued by the leaders of the Evangelical Church in Westphalia on Reformation Day (31 October) 1967. It took the form of a pamphlet called *Bibel und Bekenntnis* (Bible and Creed), of which large numbers were printed and distributed. This pamphlet began by reprinting a number of earlier views on points of theological controversy and went on to say that the leaders of the church felt bound to contradict certain contemporary theological statements 'out of a sense of responsibility for the church members entrusted to our charge, who are confused and wait for the guidance of the church's leaders'. There can be no doubt that confusion exists, but there may be a difference of opinion as to whom that confusion is due. Each party will probably ascribe the responsibility to the other and I shall not attempt to decide here who is right. In any case, the advice which the leaders of the Evangelical Church of Westphalia give in the face of this confusion is as follows (in as far as it touches on our present subject):

Theology has correctly pointed out that the resurrection of Jesus Christ cannot be proved by the methods of historical scholarship. But if from this the inference is drawn that the resurrection of Jesus Christ is neither a historical event nor a fact of redemption, but that it is merely a notion deriving from Gentile-Christian piety and only means devotion to God and his service, then it must be stated that this doctrine cannot be brought into accordance with the testimony of the resurrection of the Holy Scriptures.

I wonder whether this 'advice' is really calculated to clear up the confusion of church members?

The second declaration was made in Düsseldorf on Repentance Day (22 November) 1967 at a mass meeting of the so-called Confessional Movement, 'No Other Gospel'; it was given to the press by the Evangelical Press Agency. Our theme is treated in the Fourth Article, which runs as follows:

'But now is Christ risen from the dead!' (I Cor. 15.20). 'The Lord is risen indeed!' (from Luke 24.34). We confess the gospel that God raised Jesus bodily from the grave after his death on the cross and exalted him to be Lord. Hence we must reject the false doctrine that Jesus' body was corrupted, that he rose in a merely spiritual sense and that he only lives on impersonally, through his Word. We must also reject the false doctrine that the New Testament Easter witnesses clothed their message in mythically coloured legends, or that they did not intend to report the appearances of the risen Lord (as the basis and presupposition of faith) in the form in which they really occurred. We must reject the false doctrine that it is possible to be a disciple of the crucified without commitment to the person of the risen Lord.

Since both these statements were widely known among my hearers I could not simply ignore them. I did, however, avoid any extensive comment, preferring rather to rely on my own exegesis to refute much of what is stated in these declarations in such bold – and no doubt often unconsidered – terms. Even the concepts used are not properly clarified. In the end I deliberately decided to go into the controversy here and there. Thus a polemical note has occasionally entered into my exposition, contrary to my original intention. I hope, however, that this will not unduly disturb the reader, especially as he will probably be familiar with the present controversy about the resurrection of Jesus. I should none the less be grateful if he would concentrate on the argument as a whole, rather than on these polemical passages; I am certain that he will then find the exposition helpful.

Philosophy used sometimes to be called the handmaid of theology; I should like to put it somewhat differently: responsible theology is the handmaid of faith. A handmaid does not perform the work herself – that is the function of her master. But she clears everything out of the way which might hinder her master and holds everything in readiness, as far as possible, so that he can do his work. I cannot relieve any reader of his own act of faith in the risen Jesus of Nazareth. That is his own venture. But I can try to show what this faith looks like, I can lead up to it and in so doing can remove a number of false hindrances from the road. The 'foolishness' of faith will not be done away with in this process, as people sometimes say. On the contrary, the real foolishness stands out all the more plainly; but with it the promise which meets the venture of faith. That is what I wanted to achieve with these lectures, and that is the aim of this book.

It will again be easy to 'prove' on the basis of this piece of work that I am a 'heretic', if quotations are torn out of their context. The people who try to do so will no doubt find this the best way of bolstering up a weak argument. But they must not expect me to reply.

With regard to the book itself one point must be mentioned. It is based on the manuscript of the lectures and will sometimes noticeably be designed to be heard, not read. I have made stylistic alterations here and there, but I have not aimed at the purism of the 'written' word. Some readers will find this a fault, just as it is often felt to be a fault when a 'piece of writing' is preached. But I believe that it is easier to read the spoken word than to listen to the written one. Be that as it may, since every *Sitz im Leben* demands its own form, I should have had to rewrite the lectures entirely in order to turn them into a written essay; and for this I had neither time nor strength. But I hope that the material may make amends for any faults of presentation. The reader who concentrates on the content will hardly be much disturbed by finding the spoken word in print; nor will he miss notes and a bibliography. In my opinion, the scholarly method does not mean commenting on all previous opinions or attesting one's wide reading through voluminous notes. The man who has read everything and can quote everything is not necessarily a scholar. Scholarship means being able to grasp the essence of a problem and to present the material in logical form. This is what I have tried to do. I have deliberately omitted a bibliography, but I must not only stress but gratefully acknowledge that I am indebted to many scholars for stimulating suggestions. If a scholarly account is to be comprehensible to the layman, the method must not be any the less scholarly. On the contrary – the writer must go a step further, reducing the argument to its simplest essentials. I hope that in this I have been successful.

I should like to express my thanks to Fräulein Margitta Weitzel and Dr Johannes Lähnemann, who helped in the preparation of the manuscript and who read the proofs.

Münster W. Marxsen
2 July 1968

I The Controversy over the Resurrection of Jesus

In all the discussions which at present occupy our churches and our theology, the question of Jesus' resurrection plays a decisive part; one might even say *the* decisive part. This is understandable, particularly if we remember the Pauline statement so often quoted in this connection: 'If Christ has not been raised, then our *kerygma* (our message) is in vain and your faith is in vain' (I Cor. 15.14). According to this, talking about the resurrection means talking about the faith of the church. If Jesus' resurrection is a matter of uncertainty, faith will be a matter of uncertainty too, and in the same degree. Once this fact is recognized, the passion with which the controversy is waged becomes understandable.

There is another factor as well. According to the traditional Christian interpretation, the Christian's hope of resurrection is closely connected with the resurrection of Jesus. For instance, in the same chapter Paul calls Christ the 'first fruits' of the resurrected; that is to say, it is Christ who has begun the awaited resurrection of the dead (I Cor. 15.23).

Faith and hope: both are evidently involved. If there is uncertainty or obscurity at this point, above all if there is no longer any conviction, there is a risk of jeopardizing more or less everything to which a Christian clings.

I should like to emphasize at the very start that I can easily understand the disquiet caused by certain recent statements, although whether it is necessary is another question. We must not lay the fault primarily at the door of the people who have subjected traditional ideas and viewpoints to a critical analysis, generally in scholarly articles. The disquiet has been far more frequently caused by tearing individual sentences out of their context in articles of this kind and popularizing them. These sentences have then taken on a quite different colouring from that of their context. If they have turned into slogans this was not the fault of their authors but of the people who popularized such isolated quotations. But enough of that.

The fact of the matter is that we apparently have to do with a complex problem which has to be considered from a great many different aspects. An evaluation of the texts, their date and interpretation plays a part. Ideas belonging to the history of religion must be grasped and put in their place, for we do not meet talk of the resurrection only, or for the first time, in Christianity; it occurs much earlier. Differing traditions must then be compared and explained. And there is much else.

Just because the problem has so many different levels, discussions often quickly and unexpectedly find themselves in a *cul-de-sac*. We fumble with the different threads and soon the whole complex seems to be a skein so tangled that we despair of unravelling it. And then we are too impatient to attempt the careful unravelling necessary. Instead, we try to cut right through the knots by taking refuge in a creed, or perhaps in an argument which, though rational, cuts the corners. In this way the chance of mutual understanding is lost and instead of a conversation we are suddenly involved in a controversy. And so the quarrel is born.

This must stop. With a little goodwill, patience as cardinal virtue, and an honest attempt really to listen to one another, it ought to be possible at least to arrive, first at some degree of clarity and then at an understanding. I hope that these lectures may contribute towards this end.

It is not my intention to offer anything sensational, but it may well be that some of you will find certain ideas alien – perhaps even alienating – when you compare them with the ideas you have been familiar with up to now or with what you have assumed was a matter of certainty. If this is so, I would beg you to consider whether you cannot make any sense of these, at first sight, objectionable ideas – at least in the context of my argument. It is certainly far from my intention to destroy anyone's faith, as people call it, or even to disturb that faith. What I do want to do is to try to lead towards an understanding of faith, in so far as faith can ever be understandable.) I believe this to be of the first importance, particularly in modern controversy, for one can only answer for the faith that one understands. I mean this quite literally: only the person who understands his faith and can make it understandable to other people has an answer when he is asked what his faith is. *arguments*

It is not my intention, either, to enter into polemics, although this is a grave temptation in view of some of the things that can be heard or read today on our subject. But polemic is seldom helpful – and at most only when it helps one to define one's own position more closely and to justify it more adequately.

My real aim is to develop this apparently complicated problem as simply as possible. I am not presupposing any theological training but merely the readiness to follow the train of thought which I shall develop step by step. I must stress this point because it is not a matter of course nowadays: I want critical listeners, who will examine what I am about to say, but who will also be prepared (if they accept the logic of what they hear) to re-examine their own previous view of Jesus' resurrection and if necessary to modify it.

How, then, shall we attack the problem? This is of primary importance, since it will largely determine what follows. For that reason I am not starting from a point of controversy, since this would have to be more or less arbitrarily chosen; and our reflections must not be guided by what is merely arbitrary. Instead I shall start from a quite simple statement, one which I believe you will agree offers an obvious starting point in the case of our particular theme. The statement is: Jesus is risen.

At this point there is complete agreement. There is no Christian who would not be able to give his assent to this statement. Nor is there any theologian—irrespective of the camp or school to which he belongs – who would not agree with it. That is a point perhaps worth noting in our present situation, and this fact alone would recommend the sentence as a starting point.

The unity which may be found here is not to be underestimated, even though we must immediately add that it does not take us very far. Why not?

We could answer quickly enough by pointing out that there is a distinction between what we say and what we mean by what we say. This does not only apply to our present subject of discussion; it is true in general, even though it is a problem which is often over-looked or too quickly pushed aside in discussion. Of course when we use certain words, or when we combine certain words in a sentence, we associate these words with particular concepts. And so we are easily inclined to read our ideas into words, and to think that ours is the only correct way in which the words can be used. But it is important to realize that other people express other ideas in exactly the same words. This means that our language is not unambiguous. A further difficulty is that we ourselves do not always use the same words in the same sense. Consequently a distinction must be made between what is said and what is meant. When two people say the same thing it by no means follows that they must therefore mean the same thing; and so the same expression can sometimes actually cover up a dissension. This very thing can in fact be illustrated by our example. Our generally accepted statement 'Jesus is risen' is neces-sarily followed by the question 'what does this mean?' We must go on to define, to explain what the various concepts signify. And then the disagreement quickly shows itself.

It is not even clear what we are to understand here by 'Jesus'. Do we mean the man, Jesus of Nazareth? Or Jesus Christ? Or the Son of God? There are a number of important points to be cleared up here. But let us leave that on one side for the moment, for we could perhaps soon arrive at an understanding in the context of our statement. I shall return to this later.

Few people realize that there is also a problem inherent in the word 'is'. But here again I will just mention the point and will go into it in more detail presently.

There is no doubt at all that the most difficult problem is to say what one understands by 'risen'. Let me suggest one or two possible answers. One can, for example, add a word and interpret 'risen' as meaning 'bodily risen'; although this immediately raises the new question of what 'bodily' means. Are we to think of what is called a 'glorified' or 'spiritual' body? Or are we to think of the same body that was laid in the grave – an interpretation which raises the question of the empty tomb. One must certainly distinguish between the 'body' and the 'flesh'. We shall have to return to this point later in connection with the Pauline statements. If we interpret 'risen' in what is called a 'spiritual' sense, this gives us an entirely new starting-point. There are numerous variations here. Are we talking about the resurrection of Jesus in the hearts of his disciples? Or is Jesus risen into the proclamation of the church?

You are familiar with these answers and others like them; more might be added. But it is obvious that a dispute is bound to arise at this stage. For if when I say 'Jesus is risen' I mean 'Jesus has risen bodily from the grave', whereas another person in repeating the same sentence means that 'Jesus is risen in a spiritual sense', then we still have one simple and generally accepted sentence (there we were agreed); but what we understand by the sentence is entirely different; and thus our unity shows itself to be merely an apparent one.

There is another factor as well. Up to now we have started from our given sentence and have gone on to interpret it. We must now see that the person who repeats the sentence performs the interpretative process in reverse, so to speak. For he interprets what he thinks with the help of the sentence: what he wants to say precedes the sentence which he repeats. Briefly, the person who supports the 'physical' interpretation and believes that this is the only one which is correct, expresses this belief in the sentence 'Jesus is risen' and thinks that this sentence is a proper and adequate expression of his opinion. Consequently he will be inclined to say: 'Anyone who understands this sentence in a different sense, understands it wrongly and robs it of its essential content; and he really ought not to repeat the sentence at all.' According to this view, resurrection is indivisible from physical being; if the corporeality is suppressed, the word 'risen' is being misused. This judgment is undoubtedly correct from the standpoint of the opinion which the interpreter has incorporated in the sentence. But another person who incorporates his own, different opinion in the same sentence is right as well – from the standpoint of his own particular view.

We can see that language is a somewhat complicated affair. If we are not aware of the problem, we are easily inclined to look for the fault behind the dispute in the wrong place. The distinction between what is said and what is meant is inevitable; but on the other hand this distinction leads us into a dissension which we cannot ignore. For who is in fact really right?

It is obvious that the question has two sides to it. On the one hand there is the question of who understands the sentence from which we started in the correct sense. But then we should have to go on to decide who has the right to formulate his particular opinion with the help of this sentence. It is very important to proceed correctly at this point.

In general the procedure is as follows. One takes a third, external court of appeal: the New Testament. This is so obvious and seems so much a matter of course that one goes to work without delay. But we shall see presently that by so doing we are not making the matter any easier; on the contrary, it becomes more complicated than ever. For we can now make the astonishing observation that the representatives of widely differing schools of thought all base their views of 'risen' on the New Testament – whether rightly or wrongly remains to be seen. So the decision as to the proper interpretation would only be transferred from our own statement to the various statements of the New Testament.

Other people would proceed differently. They would, for instance, raise the question of whether resurrection is conceivable and would soon be talking (and probably incautiously) about 'modern thinking' and 'present-day experience'. They would make this the touchstone, even for the New Testament statements. The result would, of course, be disastrous and would also immediately produce the reaction: the New Testament is the Word of God and we must not judge the Word of God according to our own ideas.

It is clear, therefore, that none of these deliberations take us any further. We chose as our starting point a simple sentence, which commended itself to us because it was expressive of a consensus of opinion. But on going into it more carefully, we are faced with so many differences that we seem to have strayed into a *cul-de-sac*. There is no way out except by turning back. But would there be any point in this?

I think that there would. For if we return to our starting point once more, we can ask ourselves whether we have not made a mistake somewhere, whether we have not overlooked something in our progression from what is said to what is meant. And this proves to be exactly what has happened. For although we discovered at the beginning that every Christian could repeat the sentence 'Jesus is risen', we failed to look closely enough at the speakers themselves. Our attention was concentrated entirely on the content of the sentence and its meaning; our interest centred on that before we considered *why* the Christian really makes this statement, what ideas he associates with it and what the sentence means for him. But it is just this that must not be left out of the reckoning.

Let me show what I mean by briefly considering the word 'is', which seems to be so simple. There are two different emphases implicit in it, accents which are certainly connected and related to one another, but which must be at least distinguished if not separated from one another.

On the one hand the stress can lie on the present. If, for example, a Christian is asked why he accepts the message of Jesus (who was, after all, crucified and who lived a long time ago, among what is to us an alien people, etc.); if this man is asked why he believes that this same Jesus has something to say to him today – that even today he can come into contact with Jesus – the man can answer: 'For me, Jesus is not a figure belonging to the past; he is not a dead person but a living one. Jesus lives. He is of vital concern to me personally.' Of course, the Christian cannot prove this; but he can declare to the questioner his own involvement with the living Jesus. In this case our statement is a confession of faith, the testimony of a believer, in which the stress lies on the present.

But the stress can equally well lie on the past. In this case our sentence means, roughly speaking: the crucified Jesus is risen in the sense that after three days he rose from the dead. This happened two thousand years ago. In this case the sentence does not primarily express a personal involvement on the part of the Christian; it is simply something known to the speaker. It then has far more the character of a piece of information about a past event.

It might now be objected that such a tearing apart of the two things is inadmissible. I must again stress that this is not my intention. Of course, confession of faith in the risen Christ today has its roots in the past; and conversely, the resurrection of Jesus in the past points towards involvement, faith, today. We neither can nor should separate the one from the other. But at the same time no one will deny that a distinction between the two can be made. The question is whether the distinction is a useful one, particularly in respect of our present apparent stalemate. And I should now like to show that this is in fact the case.

One thing is evident at once. The unity which we felt to exist goes further than we first thought. Not only can all Christians join in *saying* 'Jesus is risen' (which would not mean much, as we have seen); they all *express their involvement* – that is to say their present faith – through this statement. In this sentence they all say that the Jesus who died has an immediate relevance for themselves. They confess that for them the Jesus who was once active on earth and was then crucified is not dead but alive. The fact of involvement does not *per se* presuppose unity about the means whereby this contemporary involvement was originally made possible; we do not necessarily have to agree about what started it. In other words, as long as we are stressing the implications for the *present* of the sentence 'Jesus is risen', the question of how we should think of the 'rising' as having originally taken place is no longer of decisive importance. In any case, it is impossible to deny the faith in Jesus, or involvement, of anyone for whom the statement 'Jesus is risen' is the expression of a *creed*.

But, it may be objected, those people who conceive the resurrection of Jesus in what one may briefly call physical terms might say: one certainly cannot deny someone else's faith. Even the person who 'only' accepts a 'spiritual' resurrection is 'involved' and hence a believer. But his faith has a different content and is hence a different faith.

This must be accepted for the moment. It is connected with the fact that it is possible to distinguish but not divide. But the room for the remaining divergence has been restricted. It only really emerges when we take the other aspect as starting-point, when we ask what actually happened – what the thing was in which I am still involved today. Although here the troops of opinion and counter-opinion are swiftly marshalled, the divergence no longer affects the whole sentence but only emerges at the point where we look *behind* our common, contemporary confession of faith. To put it in simple terms, the divergence lies in the fact that we give different answers to the question: what actually happened?

At this point we must try to discover whether agreement is possible and, above all, how it can be achieved.

One way is, in my opinion, closed to us. The problem cannot be solved from the starting point of contemporary faith. For although in my faith today I confess to the involvement inherent in the statement 'Jesus is risen', this faith is not capable of explaining how the 'risen' originally came about. Let me show this by putting two statements side by side and comparing them.

One man says, 'I believe, I am involved: Jesus is risen'; and he thinks of the original event in the following terms: Jesus was raised physically from the dead by God, and that fact makes it possible for me to believe in Jesus today.

Another man says, 'I believe, I am involved: Jesus is risen'; and he thinks of the original event as follows: Jesus' body remained in the grave; but Jesus was raised spiritually to new life, and that fact makes it possible for me to believe in Jesus today.

These two statements agree about the fact of involvement, but they differ in their conception of the mode of the original resurrection. It is not possible to discover who thinks correctly merely by reasoning from today's faith.

We can certainly be 'involved' once we have been informed about a past event. But our involvement cannot determine whether the information itself is true, false, or inaccurate. Many articles of the Christian faith illustrate this fact. Let me mention just one. Although I believe in Jesus, I cannot by means of this faith know that he was born of a virgin. On this point I am dependent on information. I can then incorporate this information in my faith; but my faith can neither confirm the correctness of the information, nor can it by itself (without information) deduce the content of that information. In other words, our faith, our involvement, is not an instrument of knowledge which can convey information about the past. Consequently our present involvement, which we express in the words 'Jesus is risen', is incapable of deciding anything about the mode of the resurrection. We must therefore begin in another way if we want to arrive at clarity on this question.

Since the mode belongs to the information side of our statement, we have no other choice than to look more closely at our means of information. That is to say, we must apply to our sources. Here we must distinguish between three different kinds.

You would probably not call the first source that I am about to name a source of information at all. This is understandable; and it will in any case speedily prove to be useless. But I do not want to pass it over entirely. On the contrary, I want to draw particular attention to it, not only because it has sometimes been used as a guiding line but also, and especially, because in contemporary discussion so-called modern theology is often accused of clinging to it. This source of knowledge is our own experience. We know what is possible and what is impossible according to our own experience. The resurrection of a dead person from the grave is, according to our experience, impossible. This can lead to the argument that the statement 'Jesus is risen' must on no account be interpreted as if the tomb had been empty. Our experience therefore presents us with information about the way in which the word 'risen' may be understood and the way in which it may not. Now, it is undoubtedly true that our experience tells us that a resurrection in this sense is impossible. But it is none the less inadmissible to make our (inevitably limited) experience the yardstick for what once happened and for the way in which it happened. I should like us to be quite clear about this. Whatever conclusions we may arrive at in the course of these lectures about the resurrection, they must on no account be based on the touchstone of our experience or of present-day scientific knowledge. Such a procedure would be simply unscholarly, because it would be an inadmissible coupling of two different methodological domains – the historical and the scientific. I will readily admit that such arguments are occasionally used and that sometimes statements have been so cloudily formulated as to give the impression that this argument was being used. But misunderstandings can be remedied; and that is what I am trying to do at this point. Our experience is not a source of information on which we can draw in deciding how 'risen' is to be understood.

There remain two further, closely connected sources of information. The first is probably the one most frequently used. This is information conveyed through other people. These people want us to believe that Jesus is risen. When we ask them how Jesus rose from the dead, they give us their own ideas on the subject. Generally speaking this is the method used in preaching and instruction. If faith is then kindled (through preaching, for example), this faith is subsequently associated with the particular idea of the resurrection which has been passed on to us. This (individual) conception is thus simply part of our faith from the very beginning. If someone later asserts that the 'information' side of our faith is incorrect, we are inevitably afraid that our faith as involvement will also lose its basis. This is frequently the situation out of which the present dispute about the resurrection of Jesus springs. Under this aspect the disquiet is entirely comprehensible.

But we must be clear about the fact that information about the mode of the resurrection is not an integral part of our present involvement. I have tried to show that involvement through faith can exist even when we have a completely different picture of the original mode of the resurrection. This means that even if we have to correct or modify our idea of that mode, it by no means implies the collapse of our present faith. We shall formulate our belief differently, but our faith in Jesus will not simply fall to pieces. I am laying great stress on this point because I do not want anyone who may perhaps through these lectures arrive at another view about the mode of the resurrection to fall into false anxiety and abandon not only his previous idea of the mode but his faith with it. This kind of fear, at any rate, is uncalled for.

In our context the point is this: people receive information about the mode of the resurrection at the same time as they receive the article of faith, 'Jesus is risen'; but the content of this information differs. Faith is incapable of deciding which idea is correct. But the question must none the less be decided. How is this possible?

Of course, we can say that we have such complete trust in the person who gave us the information (our priest or minister, our teacher, our church) that we are not prepared to replace the one idea by another. But we must then be clear about what we are doing. We are binding ourselves to another person's opinion. But what if his opinion is mistaken? I am far from maintaining *a priori* that this is the case. But the possibility, at least, cannot be excluded *a priori* either – especially when the problem is a disputed one. There is, after all, no doubt that the person who gave us our information received that information in his turn from someone else. That is to say, there is a chain of tradition through which the information has been passed on – a chain which can, and must, be traced back to its beginnings.

If we do this, we finally come to the third source of information, which I should for the moment like to name in quite general terms as the early texts, largely speaking those belonging to the New Testament. Of course I might have put these at once in place of the second source; for generally one turns immediately to the New Testament as soon as any doubt arises about the mode of the resurrection. I deliberately avoided doing so because I wanted to draw attention to a dependence in which we all stand but of which we are often unconscious. For we do not turn to the New Testament for information with an open mind, as we are inclined to think. We are prejudiced – prejudiced through the tradition of which we are a part; that is to say, prejudiced by the second source of information I have mentioned. This is unavoidable, but we ought to be aware of the fact. For it is now all too easy to find the opinions that we bring with us in the texts because we have unconsciously put them there. This can only be avoided to any extent at all if we are clear in advance about the preconceived interpretation with which we turn to the New Testament; and if we are also aware of the source of this preconceived interpretation, i.e., the tradition of which we are a part. The chance of as unprejudiced an enquiry as possible is only open to us if we are conscious of this preconceived interpretation and are aware of its origin and its content. For it is only when we put our questions without prejudice that we are able to hear the answer of the texts and not our own answer; and it is only then that we are capable of noticing features which diverge from the preconceived interpretation which we have brought with us.

This should by no means be taken to imply that we must immediately doubt all our previous convictions. But since the resurrection of Jesus is today a matter of dispute, the right answers must be of concern to us. We can have no interest in clinging to our own ideas, come what may, even if they prove on careful examination to be untenable.

II Later Texts on the Resurrection of Jesus

Up to now our reflections have led to one concrete question. We want to know in what sense the word 'risen' is to be understood in the credal statement 'Jesus is risen', in as far as this relates to the original resurrection. We want to know this because it is apparent that this is the point of dissension. For the sake of clarity, let me formulate the point once more in different terms. We want to test the information which has come down to us in an article of faith; we want to discover whether it is possible to agree on a common formulation of the mode of Jesus' resurrection. Furthermore, if the answer is 'yes', we want to know what the formulation must look like if we are to be able to talk appropriately about the resurrection of Jesus within the framework of the article of faith. But what right do we have to apply to the written texts for the answer?

1. THE METHODOLOGY OF TEXTUAL INVESTIGATION

One can answer this question by saying that the method is universally used – all later talk of the resurrection of Jesus takes its position from these texts, or at least claims to do so. We are therefore dealing with a consensus in practice. But is that in itself sufficient justification for proceeding in this way in our search for an answer which will be to the purpose? We must test the justifiability even of things which seem to us a matter of course. If we do not, we are making ourselves (unconsciously) all too easily dependent on prejudices, which are least recognizable as prejudices when there is such a surprising unanimity of practice. We must first, therefore, see why we use texts for the answering of our question.

There are two possible reasons. On the one hand people frequently point to the special character of the New Testament, calling it the

Word of God and perhaps even arguing from the divine inspiration of this collection of twenty-seven writings. The conclusion then is that here we are dealing with texts of a quite special kind and that for this reason we may expect them to give us the appropriate information. But at this point a fallacy easily creeps in.

When we enquire about the mode of Jesus' resurrection, we are asking about an event that occurred some time and somehow in the past. At all events, it took place *before* the New Testament writings were compiled. On this point everyone agrees, even the people who ascribe to these texts a special quality, as a starting bonus, so to speak.

But if we stop short at the texts in our enquiry, we are making them a barrier between us and the event about which we seek information. We are not taking our bearings from the event itself, but from the opinions of the authors of these particular texts. The texts may be the Word of God, or inspired, however one likes to phrase it; but if this means that we may not enquire into the events behind their statements, then the result will not be capable of convincing anyone who does not share the presupposition of inspiration. For there is no recognizably special character about the texts themselves. One ought therefore to examine the correctness of the presupposition; that is to say, one ought really to work out something like a 'doctrine of the Scriptures'. But I cannot do this within our present framework.

I am bound to point out, however, that here we are touching on a problem which has become of the greatest topical interest, and in a particular connection. In the Düsseldorf Declaration of Repentance Day, 1967, the so-called Confessional Movement 'No other Gospel' maintained, among other things, that: 'We must reject the false doctrine that the New Testament Easter witnesses . . . did not intend to report the appearances of the risen Lord . . . in the form in which they really occurred.' I shall come back to this declaration later. At the moment I am only concerned with one point. According to this sentence (which I have abridged), it is 'correct doctrine' when one stops short at the New Testament texts themselves, since these witnesses intended to report events *in the form in which they occurred*. In other words, their information is classified without further examination as being historically reliable. This is one aspect, among others, of the special character of the New Testament.

Here a question must be raised. If we make the special character of the New Testament writings our starting point and ground the reliability of the information which they give us on this fact (as the Düsseldorf Declaration does), ought we not to find an internal consistency in the writings, instead of rival or even sometimes contradictory information? Yet we shall see that the latter is exactly what we have.

But we must then go on to conclude: whatever character is ascribed to the New Testament writings, it is quite impossible to deduce from this character the reliability of the information about the mode of Jesus' resurrection. I must stress that in saying this I am saying nothing against the special character of the texts. But the special character of the New Testament cannot consist in the fact that it represents an infallible source of information, because (as I am about to show) the information which we receive from the New Testament texts in fact conflicts. Thus we cannot justify taking our bearings from the texts on the grounds that – through their special quality – they give us unmistakable and reliable information about our question.

Yet we have to work from the texts for another reason. For they are, when all is said and done, nearer to the event into which we are enquiring than we are today. They are therefore historical sources for us. It is true that one must not simply identify historical sources with the subject about which they give information. But without sources we cannot, after all, know anything at all about the past. So with our texts we have to do with an intermediate court of appeal, though with nothing more than that. The texts are indispensable, however, so we must give them our attention.

We must be clear about another point as well. Having considered why we are using texts at all, we must now examine the question of how the texts are to do what we expect of them. Here also, people frequently pass swiftly over the inherent problem and then argue too precipitately.

Let us remind ourselves that we are turning to the texts with a particular question in mind. But this does not necessarily mean that the texts, for their part, are in a position to answer this particular question. For they could in fact be intending to say something quite different. To put it in terms of our own particular problem; are the texts concerned (or, more precisely, are they *primarily* concerned) to give information about the mode of Jesus' resurrection? Or are they primarily assertions of faith? We are bound to ask this question, because the answer will largely determine the other questions which we put to the texts.

At this point we again come across the problem with which we already concerned ourselves at the beginning of the lectures. I said then that in the sentence 'Jesus is risen' we have not only to distinguish between what is said and what is meant, but that we must above all discover *why* a person makes a particular statement. For the same reason we must now clarify why the writers made statements about the resurrection of Jesus, what ideas they personally associated with the statements and what the statements meant for them. Let me formulate an alternative: did they want primarily to inform, or primarily to awaken faith? For the two purposes must be differentiated.

If the writers wanted to inform, then and only then can we put our question directly to the texts. Even in this case we shall not discover what really happened, but only what the authors of the texts think happened. We should therefore still not have arrived at our goal, even if the texts were to present us with a direct answer to our question.

We are not, indeed, debarred from putting our question, even if the texts are a call to faith – if they are intending to lead us into involvement. But it is obvious, I think, that we can then no longer put our question as directly as in the former case.

Of course one must qualify these two alternatives by adding that one must distinguish but not divide. For even if the texts are a call to faith, even if their aim is to produce involvement, they always *work through* information about the resurrection. In other words, even if they wanted to make statements of faith, the authors of the texts had a particular idea about what the resurrection of Jesus means. This must not be overlooked. But in that case, the idea takes up an entirely different position within the framework of a statement of faith; it is used, but is not the *immediate* interest of the statement.

Let me suppose for a moment (purely hypothetically) that we have to do with *statements of faith* in the New Testament texts. It is then conceivable (again we are speaking hypothetically) that the same thing happened at the time of writing as happens today: that the same phraseology was used as a call to faith or involvement; but that behind this phraseology lay different ideas about the meaning of the word 'risen'. And again, in questioning the texts, one only discovers this fact when one proceeds from what they say to what they mean. It was evidently possible even then to differ in meaning from time to time. Yet every writer considered his concept as being a call to involvement. But the same involvement could come into being with the help of different notions about the meaning of 'risen'.

One thing is now clear, I think. The problem which concerned us at the beginning of our lectures in connection with the sentence 'Jesus is risen' has now been pushed further back. It is not a specifically modern problem at all, but faces us in exactly the same way in the early texts as well.

This fact is frequently overlooked. The result is that we approach the texts with our own questions, without considering whether these texts are intending to answer them directly – or, indeed, whether they are in a position to do so. If this is not the case, we can still, of course, put our question. Basically speaking, we can put any question which is of immediate interest to ourselves to any text at all. But we must not expect that every text will be able to answer what is (from its own point of view) a purely arbitrary question. Consequently we must not simply assume that our interests coincide with those of the writer. A writer must be allowed the right to stress, bring to the fore and develop what is of most consequence to *him*; and we must not subsequently lay down the law about where his interests are to lie. This happens all too frequently, however, when questions are put directly to the texts without taking the problems we have just discussed into consideration. I imagine that everyone would agree with this in principle, although we are not, of course, thereby prejudging the intentions of the New Testament writers.

These intentions are still occasionally a matter of dispute. Did the writers mean to give information or to issue a call to faith? The answer that they wanted to do both is neat but spurious. For to say this is simply to pass over the relative importance of the two motives. The point is to decide what they *primarily* wanted to do. In order to make it clear that although I do not want to divide, we are bound to distinguish, let me formulate the point in two questions, which contain the same elements but differ in their accentuation.

Did the authors of the texts want to give information about certain past events *in order that* faith might be awakened through these events (i.e., Jesus is physically risen from the dead, and because of that fact you may today undertake the venture of faith in him)?

Or were the writers of the texts issuing a call to faith *through* certain information which they presented (i.e., you are invited to undertake the venture of faith in Jesus because he did not remain among the dead but is alive – however one may care to think of this as taking place)?

The two are not identical. But by paying due attention to the different stress, we might succeed in escaping from the dissension which exists today.

I am not now proposing to settle in advance the dispute about what the writers of our New Testament texts primarily had in mind. This would be to run the risk of committing ourselves to a particular path, of making mistakes in the framing of our questions and of deciding on the result in advance. Consequently I do not propose to begin with the New Testament itself. Instead I shall turn to a text whose very wording precludes any doubt about its intention: what is known to us as the Apostles' Creed.

2. THE APOSTLES' CREED

The Apostles' Creed starts off three times with the words 'I believe' – at least by implication, though the second article is covered (under the conjunction 'and') by the 'I believe' of the opening. It is therefore intended as a confession or statement of faith. There is no doubt that this is its main emphasis.

Today we know that the Apostles' Creed came into being gradually. Many stages in its evolution are known, early forms reaching back into the second century and joining up with New Testament formulations. But this history does not concern us here; and we shall also ignore the question of the mutual relation of the three articles. Our prime concern is with one of the statements in the second article – the statement about the resurrection. We must look at it in its context, because the context can indicate the way in which we are to assess the statement.

The second article runs:

And [I believe] in Jesus Christ his only Son our Lord, who was conceived by the Holy Ghost, born of the Virgin Mary, suffered under Pontius Pilate, was crucified, dead and buried, he descended into hell; the third day he rose again from the dead, he ascended into heaven, and sitteth on the right hand of God the Father Almighty; from thence he shall come to judge the quick and the dead.

First, let us look at the syntax of this second article within the framework of the creed as a whole. The creed starts three times with the words 'I believe'. This belief is directed towards God the Father; towards Jesus Christ, his only Son our Lord; and towards the Holy Ghost. These three points of reference of the one faith (God, Jesus, the Spirit) are then developed separately, in the case of the second article through what is, practically speaking, a relative clause. This relative clause lists what are sometimes called 'the facts of redemption': conceived by the Holy Ghost, born of the Virgin Mary, suffered under Pontius Pilate, crucified, dead and buried, descended into hell, the third day rose again from the dead, ascended into heaven, sitteth on the right hand of God, from thence he shall come for judgment.

Now there can be no doubt that these so-called facts of redemption are arranged in a certain order; that is to say, they are named in a series which can be interpreted (and which the authors of the creed probably meant to be interpreted) as a sequence of events. In this sequence the first 'facts of redemption' refer to the past (from the conception to the ascension); then comes the present ('sitteth on the right hand of God'); and finally there is a glance at the future (his coming again for judgment). But all together, as we have said, they are grouped, practically speaking, into a relative clause which defines the object of the creed's faith more exactly. Let us be more precise: the faith of the creed is directed towards Jesus, who is more closely designated (before the beginning of the relative clause) by two titles – God's 'only son' and 'our Lord'; the designation of Jesus as Christ will hardly have been considered as a title, but as part of the name. Now, the second title underlines the fact that we are dealing with a confession of *faith*, for to call Jesus our Lord is to express involvement. The person who is my Lord is of intimate concern to me.

If we now look at this second article of the creed in the context of what we said before, we shall discover that here we have the two different stresses which we wanted to distinguish but not divide, in a specially pronounced form. At the beginning involvement is stressed: I believe in Jesus Christ, (God's) only Son, our Lord. The relative clause then follows with 'information' about the Jesus to whom faith is directed. Here it is particularly noticeable that the individual pieces of information are only loosely linked with faith. There is not merely distinction but almost division, for we confess faith in Jesus, God's only Son, our Lord; then, in the relative clause, this Jesus, to whom this faith is directed, is more closely described. It seems to me important to draw attention to the fact that the very wording of this article shows that the individual statements are not made because we believe or ought to believe in *them* but because they describe *the being* in whom we believe. To that extent, although these individual statements apply to Jesus, they are not themselves what are sometimes called articles of faith. The two things must be distinguished. The Apostles' Creed is not concerned with faith in the virgin birth, the death of Jesus, the resurrection, etc.; it is concerned only with *faith in Jesus*, who is more closely described in the relative clause through the account of the path he took. Whether and how these so-called facts of redemption must be believed in as such apart from the Apostles' Creed need not concern us here. We shall discuss this point later in asking whether belief in the resurrection is possible or necessary.

It may seem surprising that in this interpretation of the creed, the statement 'the third day he rose again from the dead' moves still further away from the context of faith than it did in our previous discussion. But for all that, it can be clearly demonstrated that this interpretation is not a false one. Let us look at the preceding statement, 'suffered under Pontius Pilate, was crucified, dead, and buried'. We must be careful here not to be too hasty with our own ideas. We understand Jesus' death as a saving death and his cross, therefore, as a saving event. But there is nothing about that here. Here the facts are simply reported. Many other people may have suffered, been crucified, dead and buried under Pontius Pilate. And no more is reported even of Jesus, although long before the creed was drawn up, other Christian documents (Paul's letters, for example) speak of Jesus' death as a redeeming death. The Apostles' Creed, however, is silent on this point. Later, this was felt to be a lack and what is known as the Nicene Creed, which reflects a somewhat later development, has 'was crucified *for us* under Pontius Pilate'. This 'for us', which claims an actual, verifiable death as a saving one, is missing in the Apostles' Creed.

From this, however, we can see how the individual parts of the relative clause are meant to be understood: as a description of Jesus' progress. We do not learn what interpretation is to be put on 'the third day he rose again from the dead', because these are mere words. But the context gives certain indications which at least take us a step further. We might put it as follows: 'the third day he rose again from the dead' is the expression of a *happening* which took place between the crucifixion, the descent into hell and the ascension. Nor is it a happening which is (at least in this context) especially singled out. It is not a central event on the path of Jesus, though it is a necessary one, which forms a bridge between the once dead and now living Jesus, who 'sitteth on the right hand of God'.

It would be dangerous to speak here of a 'historical event', for the ideas which we now associate with this concept were then unknown. We shall return to the problems associated with this point later. For the moment let me simply say in general terms that according to the Apostles' Creed 'the third day he rose again from the dead' was a *real event* on the path which Jesus trod. In conjunction with the other events, we are here being *informed* about Jesus' resurrection. This information is prompted by two different motives, which are, however, closely bound up with one another. On the one hand the information is given *so that* we may find faith in Jesus who, through these events, arrived at the right hand of God and is therefore 'our Lord'. But it is also given in order to explain *why* we should have faith in Jesus – the reason being, because he trod this path.

Thus although the Apostles' Creed speaks of Jesus' resurrection on the third day as if it were an event which actually took place, this must not lead us to a premature conclusion. For it would certainly be premature if we were now to say: the resurrection of Jesus must have been a real event, for this early text says so. Here we have to distinguish. Up to now our conclusions have only taken us as far as the convictions of the people who formulated the creed. But do these convictions coincide with the truth? Are we really dealing with an event?

We must not call everyone who asks this question a sceptic. It is true that this reproach is frequently levelled, but it does not become the more justifiable through constant repetition. We cannot seriously deny that it is one thing to *know* about an event, and another to be (merely) *convinced* that it took place. The two only coincide (at least more or less) when we have to do with an eyewitness account of the event in question; and no one would maintain that the authors of the Apostles' Creed were eyewitnesses. We are therefore bound to ask: how did they arrive at their conviction? Or in other words: who told them before they could tell us?

In principle we shall have to put this question to all the texts (not only to the Apostles' Creed) as long as we cannot be certain that they derive from eyewitnesses of the event. Sometimes it will be impossible to find an answer, because no earlier texts are extant. This presents us with a special problem which I shall have to go into later; for we shall, in fact, come across sources behind which one can go no further – or at least only by taking into account a great number of different factors. But we have not yet arrived at this point. Meanwhile, there can be no doubt about the fact that the authors of the Apostles' Creed (and I must stress again that the creed in its present form grew gradually and was not conceived at a single stroke) were themselves informed by other people. Who were they?

We have seen that the various stages on Jesus' path are listed in order in the relative clause of the second article. This fact could immediately provide an answer to the question of who supplied the information: it came from the Gospels. The answer is undoubtedly correct. Of course it is impossible to know whether other sources, no longer extant, also existed at that time. If this were the case, the possibility of a full investigation would be denied to us. But there is no doubt at all that the New Testament Gospels were known at that time. The four canonical Gospels were circulating among Christians from the middle of the second century; and our present version of the Apostles' Creed is later than that. So we may presuppose knowledge of these four Gospels at least.

We are then faced with the question of how these Gospels were used. Formally speaking, one might say that the Apostles' Creed is a synthesis of the four Gospels, though this statement needs further clarification.

We are in fact dealing with a synthesis, because by no means all the events mentioned in the relative clause of the second article of the creed are found in all the Gospels. Mark and John know nothing of Jesus' birth, for instance (i.e., that he was 'conceived by the Holy Ghost' and 'born of the Virgin Mary'); and Matthew, Mark and John know nothing of Jesus' ascension. (We shall later see that Mark 16.9-20 was not originally a part of the Gospel.) But a question mark must be added even to the notion of a synthesis, for John's Gospel contains the concept of the pre-existence of Jesus Christ, that is to say, the idea of his existence in heaven with God before his birth. If we were really dealing with a synthesis, then it is this statement which ought to usher in the relative clause. This is the case in certain of the older Eastern symbols or creeds, which speak of the begetting of the Logos by the Father before the creation of the world, before they mention Jesus' birth from the Virgin Mary. But the Apostles' Creed is silent on this point. Hence the information given in the relative clause of the second article is at most a selective synthesis – unless, indeed, one assumes that the authors were guided by Luke's Gospel for the most part.

But even if this were so, something has been added. The synthesis does not confine itself entirely to the Gospels – not even entirely to Luke's Gospel. For nowhere in the Gospels is there any mention of the descent into hell. In our present context there is no need for me to go into the meaning of this idea. The reference is to Jesus' descent into Hades (the place of the dead or the shades of the dead, i.e., not hell in our sense of the word). The texts (and translations) differ at this point. I Peter 3.19 may probably be taken to be the source of this statement. This would confirm our conclusion that the second article was intended to list the stages of Jesus' progress. It was supposed to give a chronological list of events, by collecting and ordering information from the New Testament. The resurrection is thus only one (and by no means a particularly prominent) stage on the road which Jesus took.

3. THE GOSPELS

Let us now retrace our steps – and that means going back to the Gospels. We then find ourselves faced with the question whether the same thing is to be met with here, especially since we obviously have the description of a course of events. Jesus' resurrection is mentioned as part of this description. Is the description also concerned to give information? And are we given more exact information about the 'risen' Christ than is offered by the Apostles' Creed, which, after all, only indicates the genuinely historical character of the event without entering more particularly into its mode of operation? How does this information relate to faith, which was certainly also the concern of the evangelists?

Naturally all these questions cannot be answered in advance. We must look at the texts in more detail. This time we have the advantage that we are no longer dealing with a single text but with four parallel ones. Hence we have, of course, the chance of possibly arriving at a much fuller picture.

Unfortunately I am bound to damp these hopes somewhat, for one can only speak of parallel texts up to a certain point. They are in fact partly dependent on one another, and one must constantly be alive to this fact. One often hears the argument: 'Since we are dealing with reports from four different witnesses, it is impossible to doubt the factual nature of the happenings.' But this argument could only be used (if at all) if we had to do with independent witnesses. And this is not the case. In the present context 1 cannot prove this in detail. But I must stress that I am not putting forward my own hypothesis here – a hypothesis which you would have to accept more or less on trust. Here we have to do with a practically undisputed conclusion of Protestant and (nowadays) Roman Catholic scholarship, known as the 'two-source theory'. According to this, Mark's Gospel is the oldest. (In fact we do not know the names of any of the authors of the Gospels, as they have all come down to us in anonymous form. So the names must always be thought of in inverted commas, and in using them I am simply indicating the author of a particular work, whom we can no longer name exactly.) Matthew and Luke knew Mark's work and used it, particularly to the extent of following its general plan. In addition, both had as a second source what is known as the Logia source or 'Q' (from the German *Quelle*, or source), a collection of sayings, largely the sayings of Jesus. This source is no longer extant, but it can be reconstructed with some degree of certainty. Finally, Matthew and Luke used a certain amount of supplementary material. The two-source theory can therefore be represented as follows:

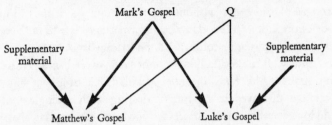

'Q' plays no part in the treatment of our theme because (here again scholars are largely agreed) it contained neither a Passion nor an Easter account. (For this reason there is a thinner line from 'Q' to Matthew and Luke in our diagram.) What is important for our purpose is that Matthew and Luke both knew and used Mark's account of the Passion and the Easter events when they compiled their own. But they expanded Mark, using other traditions (supplementary material).

The only Gospel texts, therefore, which we can really designate as parallel in the framework of our present enquiry are Mark and John, although John's Gospel is about thirty years later than Mark's, which was written shortly before AD 70. It is in any case highly improbable that the author of the Fourth Gospel knew any of the others. He certainly did not make any use of them.

Having said all this, we must go on to modify it somewhat. We can assume that the evangelists Matthew and Luke were definitely not eyewitnesses of the events they describe; if they had been, they would hardly have depended to such an extent on other sources. In spite of this we cannot simply exclude them from our enquiry, for the following reason. It is true that both are dependent on Mark; so their texts are obviously later. But this does not mean that the expansions of their source which they introduce from the supplementary material must also be later. This material could, in certain circumstances, even be very much older than Mark's Gospel. The author of the earliest Gospel either did not know the supplementary material (which could easily be the case, especially since our means of communication were lacking in those days); or he did not want to make use of it, for some reason or other.

Although we have not yet begun to talk about the texts themselves at all, what we have said can lead us to a methodological inference: we must distinguish between the date of a text and the date of the tradition which is contained in this text. It is entirely possible for relatively early traditions to be accessible only in much later textual contexts. To take a particular case, the additions to the Marcan copy made by Matthew and Luke (i.e., from supplementary material) could contain early traditions. They could, but do not necessarily do so. For of course the later alterations and expansions could equally well be the work of the evangelists themselves. Which of the two alternatives is correct must be decided in each individual case, although I must stress that certainty is not always to be achieved. One must be quite clear about the fact that some uncertainties have to be put up with! The important thing is to give them their proper name and not to try to build a firm structure on the basis of hypotheses. And the person who arrives at a different conclusion must realize that he, too, is only starting from a hypothesis.

I will point out the various places where uncertainties of this kind exist, though I shall usually avoid going into the hypotheses involved. But, someone may object, how can our problem be solved at all if such uncertainties remain? I hope to be able to show that a solution is still possible. A text is often open to various different interpretations; hence certain points must remain unsettled. But we cannot wait to answer the question of Jesus' resurrection until scholars have arrived at agreement about matters of detail.

The order in which to approach the texts emerges from what we have just said. Since we started with the Apostles' Creed, we could work backwards. This is not advisable, however, because it would then be difficult to recognize the individual character of the different Gospels. So we shall start with the oldest of the Gospels, paying particular attention to the variations in the later ones.

It is in the nature of our theme that we should address ourselves primarily to the final sections of the Gospels, but we must not overlook the fact that these concluding portions also belong in a context. If we look at this context we shall at once discover an essential difference between the Apostles' Creed on the one hand and all the Gospels on the other. The Apostles' Creed does not expend a single word on the public ministry of Jesus. In tracing Jesus' path, it immediately jumps from his birth to his sufferings under Pontius Pilate. This presents us with a question which I will at least touch on here, because we ought to be aware of the problem which we shall have to go into in more detail, though only at a later stage.

I said that the Apostles' Creed is a confession of faith in Jesus Christ, God's only Son, our Lord, and that it describes Jesus more closely by describing the path he took. But the question is: what is belief in Jesus? What does being committed to him, or being involved, really mean? It remains a purely formal statement so long as one does not explain how the *content* of faith in Jesus is to be formulated. This question is all the more pressing because, although the Apostles' Creed does not describe the road of Jesus as a precisely everyday one, it is not depicted as a path of salvation in the sense that 'for you' or 'for us' is part of the picture. Not even the fact that Jesus is now sitting at the right hand of God and can hence be acknowledged as 'our Lord', not even the expectation of his second coming as judge, can offer any closer definition of the substance of faith in Jesus. Thus the Apostles' Creed is impoverished compared with the Gospels, for they show what involvement with Jesus substantially looks like. This is what emerges from the account of his earthly ministry. Here we are shown in vivid terms what involvement with Jesus once actually looked like – and no doubt what it ought to look like still.

At this point let us recall the sentence from which we started: Jesus is risen. If this sentence (understood as a confession of faith) is to express contemporary involvement with Jesus, the content of this involvement must be filled in; otherwise the statement remains a form. But where is this essential content to be found? Must we not go back to the beginning of the Gospels, to the public ministry of Jesus?

As I have said, we shall have to discuss this point in more detail.

But perhaps we may at least assume the following: since all the Gospels mention the resurrection of Jesus, the resurrection is surely intended to be (at least among other things) the basis for contemporary involvement with Jesus (he is risen); so the previous account of Jesus' ministry is evidently designed to unfold the content of this involvement. But this would mean that the Gospel message of the resurrection does not merely begin at the point where the resurrection itself is the theme; it begins much earlier. It is certainly the past which is described at the beginning of the Gospels, but the point of the description is to show in concrete terms what faith in Jesus ought to look like today. At the end we are then told why these past events are still binding on us today: Jesus is risen.

But let us break off these reflections. They are intended merely to indicate that we must not lose sight of the context of the Easter stories. Each Gospel depicts a unity, and must not be arbitrarily chopped up into pieces; we must never forget this, even when we are concentrating on the problem presented by one particular section.

With this proviso, let us now look at the final chapters of the Gospels. In the context of our present enquiry, we are turning to them for information. We shall try to determine the concept of resurrection which prompted the evangelists in their accounts, when they wanted to arouse faith in Jesus in their own time.

I shall assume for the purposes of the discussion that the closing sections of the Gospels are, largely speaking, familiar. In my exposition I shall be drawing your attention to certain points to which I shall return later; so that the significance of some features, which seem at first sight to be unimportant, will only emerge afterwards.

(a) The Gospel of Mark

The earliest of the Gospels has the shortest account of the Resurrection. We learn that certain women saw Jesus' crucifixion from afar, among them Mary Magdalene, Mary the mother of James and Joses, and Salome (15.40f.). Then we are told of the burial at the hands of Joseph of Arimathea, Mary Magdalene and Mary the mother of Joses looking on (15.47). This takes place on the day of preparation for the sabbath. On the day after the sabbath (i.e., the third day after the Friday, according to Jewish reckoning) the three women bring spices in order to anoint the body (after burial). They go to the tomb early in the morning. After they have wondered (though only on the way, oddly enough) who was going to roll the stone away from the entrance to the tomb, they are surprised to find that the stone has already been moved. They are therefore able to enter the tomb without hindrance. They do so, find there a young man in a long white garment, and are terrified. The young man speaks to them, calming their fears, and then says: 'You seek Jesus of Nazareth, who was crucified. He has risen, he is not here; see the place where they laid him.'

It is worth noting that the resurrection is mentioned before attention is drawn to the empty tomb. We shall see later that this sequence is not without importance.

The young man now commands the women to tell the disciples and Peter that Jesus goes before them to Galilee and that they will see him there, as he had told them (cf. 14.28). The women flee from the tomb with 'trembling and astonishment'. They say nothing to anyone, thus disobeying the command given to them by the young man (whom we are undoubtedly intended to think of as an angel).

At this point (16.8) the Marcan text breaks off. What follows (16.9-20) is a later addition which is not found in all the manuscripts. This addition is a harmonization from the other Gospels. Some manuscripts have a shorter conclusion; some end altogether at 16.8. Scholars agree that the Marcan text has only been preserved as far as 16.8. The additions are expansions by another hand. But there is disagreement about the question whether Mark meant to finish his Gospel at 16.8, or whether an original, Marcan conclusion has been detached for some reason or other. I myself think that the latter is unlikely, but let us leave the question open. It is in any case certain that the Marcan text stops at 16.8.

We can then go on to establish provisionally that according to Mark the empty tomb is an integral part of the whole idea of the resurrection. This can be gathered ~~not only~~ from the last eight

verses, but also from the fact that from the time of Jesus' crucifixion the account is focused on the tomb through the two previous
mentions of the women. Admittedly this positive observation must
be balanced by two negative ones. We learn nothing about the
resurrection itself. The young man speaks of it merely as having
happened and then points to the empty tomb. Nor do we learn
anything about what is usually called the resurrection body. We
should know more if Mark had given us an account of any of
the appearances of the risen Jesus. The mode of the appearance
might then have suggested some conclusion about the nature of
the body. But since there is only the announcement of a future
meeting in Galilee (16.7), nothing more can be ascertained.

We ought now to go on to consider the question of the function
of this closing section in the framework of the Gospel as a whole.
But if I were to do this, I should have to enter the realm of
conjecture, since up to now scholars have been unable to agree on
this point. So I shall now break off the account of Mark's Gospel.
We shall come back to it in discussing the question whether the
tomb was empty or not. One answer, at least, can be considered
as certain: Mark was convinced that it was. And we might add
that the other evangelists were equally sure, for all of them mention
the empty tomb.

Of course we must note (on the basis of the two-source theory)
that here Matthew and Luke derive from Mark. To this extent
they are not primary witnesses. But they do not simply copy their
Marcan text as it stands. Let us look at the alterations and try to
explain them.

(b)   The Gospel of Matthew

After Jesus' crucifixion three women are again named as having
looked on. The names are not quite the same as those in Mark.
Instead of Salome, the mother of the sons of Zebedee is mentioned
(27.56). The laying of the body in the tomb is then watched by
Mary Magdalene and the other Mary, as in Mark.

What follows (27.62-66) is an expansion compared with Mark.
The day after the day of preparation (i.e., on the Sabbath) the

chief priests and the Pharisees go to Pilate, point out that Jesus had prophesied that he would rise from the dead after three days, and ask Pilate to have the tomb guarded, lest the disciples should come and steal the body, afterwards saying that Jesus has risen from the dead; this deception would be worse than the first. Pilate accordingly gives the chief priests and the Pharisees a guard. They all go to the tomb, secure it and seal the stone. All this takes place on the sabbath.

After this (28.1-8) Matthew again takes up the Marcan thread, though with characteristic variations. *Two* women go to the tomb (Mary Magdalene and the other Mary). Their intention is not to anoint the body (as in Mark); they simply want to see the tomb. There is accordingly no mention of their having brought spices; and of course, since they are not planning to enter the tomb, they do not wonder on the way who will roll away the stone for them. While the women are at the tomb there is an earthquake. An angel of the Lord descends from heaven, rolls away the stone and sits upon it. The guards are terrified and fall down as if dead. The angel turns to the women with words similar to those in Mark:

'Do not be afraid; for I know that you seek Jesus who was crucified. He is not here; for he has risen, as he said. Come, see the place where he lay. Then go quickly and tell his disciples that he has risen from the dead, and behold, he is going before you to Galilee; there you will see him. Lo, I have told you.'

We are not told that the women went into the tomb but we are no doubt intended to suppose that they at least looked in. The story goes on to say that the women ran quickly away from the tomb 'with fear and great joy' to tell the disciples.

Let me interrupt the story for a moment. If, in view of the two stories of the empty tomb in Mark and Matthew, we ask whether we have to do with eyewitnesses, we soon find ourselves in difficulties. Both can hardly be eyewitness accounts, for (to mention only some of the differences) either the women wanted to anoint the body and bought spices for the purpose, or they wanted to visit the tomb. Either they found the stone already rolled away, or it was rolled away in their presence through heavenly intervention. Either they found the young man in the tomb, or an angel sat on the stone in front of the tomb. And so we might go on. These are not merely unimportant features, which might be depicted differently by different narrators, according to the position from which they experienced the event. These stories cannot be harmonized and the differences cannot be simply brushed aside as unimportant, if one starts at all to go into the question of what really happened.

Now it remains conceivable, theoretically speaking, that Matthew was the better informed (because he may have had additional eyewitness accounts at his disposal). In this case one must be consistent and subject Mark's account to historical criticism. But this theory is not probable; for since we know that Matthew was familiar with Mark's Gospel down to 16.8 we must be prepared for his own systematic alteration of the copy. We can say this with the more certainty since we know (and can easily establish by comparing the texts) that Matthew made deliberate alterations in nearly every passage that he took over from Mark. The question is: can one explain the alterations?

I should like to point out three things. First, there is a reflective element here. In Palestine it would be impossible to undertake the anointing of a body on the third day, for the process of mortication would have already begun. Consequently Matthew strikes out this feature of his copy. (This of course means posing the question to Mark's text of whether the women could really have intended to anoint the body at all.) Then, we know (though admittedly only from the very much later Gospel of Peter) that there were traditions which spoke of a heavenly intervention at the tomb. We may ask whether Matthew knew such traditions and wove them into his narrative. But the reverse process is undoubtedly possible as well – that the author of the Gospel of Peter was familiar with Matthew's Gospel, among other things. In this case the writer's intention would be to accentuate the miraculous element in the story. Finally, however (and this is, as we shall see, the most important alteration), Matthew links the story of the empty tomb with what has gone before and with what follows, forming a continuous narrative; and he does this by mentioning that the guards (who had been introduced earlier) fell down as if dead.

Let us now follow up the sequel. First there is a meeting between the women and Jesus (28.9-10). He greets them. They fall before him and take hold of his feet as a sign of reverence. Jesus speaks to them but only repeats what the angel had already told them and what they were just about to do (according to 28.8): to tell Jesus' brethren (by which the disciples are meant) that they should go to Galilee, where they would see him.

Following on this, the story of the guard is brought to an end (28.11-15). The men go into the city and tell the chief priest of all people (we must remember that they were Romans!) everything that has happened – although they had fallen down as if dead. The chief priests consult with the elders as to what is to be done. They bribe the guard, who are now to tell Pilate that they had fallen asleep while on duty and that the disciples had meanwhile come and stolen the body. Here, at the very latest, the story as an account of a real event breaks down. How can anyone say what happened while he was asleep? This is the question that bothers us. But Matthew himself gives the reason why he introduces the story of the guard, which appears in none of the other Gospels. The theft of the body 'has been spread among the Jews to this day' (28.15). In other words, this is a defence. Down to the time of the evangelists (i.e., until the eighties) the fabrication that the body had been stolen was the form taken by Jewish polemic against the Christian resurrection claim. (We shall find traces of the Jewish assertion in John's Gospel as well.)

Whatever attitude one may adopt as regards the empty tomb, one thing is certain: it is an irrelinquishable part of Matthew's view of the resurrection. His defence against the Jews makes that plain.

Did Matthew himself invent the story of the guard at the tomb, which he introduces into his Marcan copy at two places (27.62-66 and 28.4) and which he later goes on to finish (28.11-15)? Or was he taking over a tradition? The answer to this question is one of the uncertainties I mentioned earlier; it is not clear. For our problem, however, the point is of no consequence, for, in view of the inner contradictions, the story cannot in any case have actually taken place as it stands.

I should now like to turn to the great closing scene of the Gospel (28.16-20). The eleven disciples go into Galilee, to the mountain where Jesus had commanded them to go. (Although Jesus had not in fact told them to go to a mountain at all, but only into Galilee in general.) There they see him and fall before him, although we are told that some of them doubted. The so-called missionary charge follows. It begins with Jesus' proclaiming the power that has been given to him: 'All authority in heaven and on earth has been given to me.' This must be understood to mean that the power was conferred only after the resurrection, since what Jesus now says is obviously intended to be new to the disciples. The eleven are now to make disciples of all nations, by baptizing them in the name of the Father and of the Son and of the Holy Ghost and by teaching them to keep all Jesus' commands. The charge closes with a word of promise: 'Lo, I am with you always, to the close of the age' (i.e., until the end of this world).

One thing becomes quite clear here. We are to become disciples of the risen Jesus. And we become so through baptism and by practising what Jesus commanded. The content of what is meant by faith in Jesus is therefore given us; and it takes its bearings from the ministry, and especially the preaching, of the earthly Jesus. We shall have to take note of this point for our subsequent discussions.

There is now absolutely no doubt that several earlier traditions have been fused together in these last five verses of Matthew's Gospel. Thus the scene seems to have been originally set on a mountain; and it is Matthew who first locates this mountain in Galilee. One could point to other inherent discords. But up to now scholars have not been able to reach agreement about the line of demarcation between Matthew and the older traditions, and we

shall again avoid entering into speculation. What *Matthew* wants
to say is in any case clear enough: if one wants to become a
disciple of Jesus today – if the claim to one's discipleship is made
at all – it is because Jesus rose from the grave, leaving his tomb
empty, and appeared first to two women and finally to his eleven
disciples. The essence of discipleship (in the terminology which we
used earlier we could also say: the essence of post-Easter involvement with Jesus) consists in the fact that one commits oneself to
what the earthly Jesus 'commanded'. Of course Matthew has a
particular idea of what the foundation which makes contemporary
involvement possible looks like. He can even summon up apolo-
getics in defence of his view where it is in dispute. But his essential
concern is that the discipleship of the earthly Jesus should be
carried forward *today*. The ending of his work makes this unmistakably clear – whatever traditions he may or may not have
used in the composition of his closing scene.

(c) The Gospel of Luke

In our examination of the contents of the third Gospel we shall
again use Mark to bring out the work's special features; for Mark
formed Luke's copy. But we shall not ignore Matthew's Gospel.
It is true that Luke almost certainly did not know Matthew's work.
But he could have picked up traditions which Matthew also knew
and incorporated in his Gospel. And of course we must compare
these.

Again, women are named as being witnesses of the crucifixion
(23.49), but their names are not given, or at least not at this point.
The women are not alone; they are together with 'all his [Jesus']
acquaintances'; and we are told that the women had followed
Jesus from Galilee. Joseph of Arimathea sees to the burial (23.50-53),
the women looking on. Luke again mentions that they had come
from Galilee with Jesus (23.55). They return to the city and immediately begin to prepare spices and ointments (not just on the day
after the Sabbath, as in Mark). But they do nothing on the Sabbath
itself. They rest, in accordance with the Jewish law (23.56).

Let me anticipate a little. At the end of the story of the empty tomb which follows, the women are named (24.10): Mary Magdalene, Joanna, Mary the mother of James, and others. If we take these passages together it is possible to gather an indication of Luke's method of procedure and hence of his intention. He links the Easter stories with Jesus' ministry in Galilee by making the Galilee group witnesses of the events in Jerusalem. Thus he introduces Joanna here (contrary to the text he is copying), she having been previously named (in 8.3) as a disciple of Jesus. She is one of several women who (according to 8.2) followed Jesus together with the twelve. This link is deliberate and hence worthy of note.

Now let us look at 24.1-11. On the first day of the week the women came with their spices to the tomb and find the stone rolled away. They enter the tomb but do not find the body there and are 'perplexed'. Then two men clothed in shining garments approach them. The women are terrified and bow their faces to the ground. The men say to them: 'Why do you seek the living among the dead? [He is not here, but has risen.] Remember how he told you, while he was still in Galilee, that the Son of man must be delivered into the hands of sinful men, and be crucified, and on the third day rise.' The women now remember Jesus' words; they go away from the tomb and tell the eleven disciples and the others all that has happened. At this point, as we have said, three of the women who tell the story to the apostles are named, although we are told that there were more than just these three. The apostles, however, do not believe; they think that what the women say is 'an idle tale'.

The Marcan source is visible through the Lucan account at many points, but none the less very considerable alterations have been made. Thus the women first discover that the tomb is empty; only then is it explained to them why this is so. The order of events therefore differs from that of Mark. What the two men say sounds like a reproach and is probably so intended. Jesus had, after all, prophesied his resurrection while he was in Galilee. The fact that the women come to the tomb shows that they did not believe Jesus, or misunderstood him. After they remember and bring the message to the apostles, they are met there too with unbelief. The finding of the empty tomb therefore does not produce faith.

A further point is also worthy of note. In Mark the young man tells the women to send the disciples and Peter to Galilee, where they will see Jesus. In the Marcan text as we have it no meeting in Galilee follows (though it does in Matthew). Luke now transforms this pointing forward to Galilee into a reminiscence of Galilee (where Jesus had already announced his coming resurrection). We can also see that Luke's changes were deliberate because all the following events are localized, not in Galilee but in and round Jerusalem. In this way it is possible for the women to meet the disciples forthwith.

The following verse (24.12) is textually disputed. It is missing in many manuscripts. According to this verse Peter ran to the tomb (in spite of the unbelief mentioned in 24.11 – or perhaps because of it), looked in, saw only the grave-clothes and went away wondering – but without arriving at belief. Since there is a reminiscence here of John 20.3-10, it has been postulated that this verse is a later addition. Other scholars have thought it possible that Luke wrote the verse himself and that it was omitted by a scribe. The general rule in such cases is: it is easier to assume that scribes have added a verse (especially for the sake of harmonizing with other texts) than that they have omitted one. But since there are of course exceptions to the rule, complete certainty is not always possible. In any case it may be said that whether Peter was at the empty tomb or not, the empty tomb did not induce belief.

But how, then, according to Luke, is faith arrived at? This is a very curious feature. Luke goes on to tell the story of the disciples on the road to Emmaus (24.13-35). On the same day (i.e., on the first day of the week, Sunday) two of the disciples (one of whom, Cleopas, is named) meet Jesus on the road to Emmaus, two hours' journey from Jerusalem; they meet but do not recognize him. He joins in their conversation and they tell him why they are so sad: Jesus of Nazareth had shown himself to be a prophet mighty in deed and in word, so that they had hoped that it was he who was to redeem Israel; but now he had been crucified. They had been astonished by certain women who had been to the tomb and had not found the body, but had seen an angel who had told them that Jesus was alive. Some of them had then gone to the tomb themselves and had found that what the women had said was true; but they had not seen Jesus. Jesus now teaches the disciples from the Scriptures, explaining that Christ had to suffer and enter into his glory. They arrive at their destination and the disciples beg their companion, who is preparing to go further, to stay with them because it is evening. Their companion assumes the position of head of the family (although as guest this is not his place), takes the bread, gives thanks, breaks it and gives it to them. Then the eyes of the disciples are opened and they recognize Jesus. But he immediately vanishes. The disciples at once start off for Jerusalem because they naturally want to tell the others of their experience as soon as possible. But at first they do not find an opportunity, for the eleven and the others who are assembled in Jerusalem take the words out of their mouths, so to speak, with the announcement: 'The Lord is risen indeed, and has appeared to Simon.' Only then can the Emmaus disciples recount their experience.

There is no parallel to this story in any other of the Gospels. Why, we shall only be able to say when we have completed our review. But I should like to point to one feature at the outset. There is evidently a particular reason why the eleven and the others who are assembled with them anticipate the Emmaus disciples: the priority of Jesus' appearance to Peter is to be brought out and guaranteed. This is important because we have here a parallel to I Cor. 15.3ff., where Paul names Peter as the first of the witnesses to whom Jesus appeared. But this is the case in none of the other Gospels. In Mark no appearances are mentioned at all. In Matthew Jesus appears first to the two women at the tomb and then to the eleven in Galilee; there is no mention of a special appearance to Peter. In John, as we shall see, Jesus appears first to Mary Magdalene, although it is Peter who is the first to believe. It is only Luke of all the evangelists who mentions an appearance to Simon Peter first of all.

What is striking is the method. This verse (24.34) has the effect

of a deliberate correction. As we have seen, it interrupts the flow
of the original story. If one looks at the Greek text, one discovers
that the turn of phrase is a stylized one – a kind of formalized
creed, which has a close verbal similarity to I Cor. 15.5. It is therefore a justifiable inference that this verse did not originally belong
to the story of the disciples on the road to Emmaus but was
inserted later. Whether it was inserted by Luke or by an earlier
hand we cannot be sure. But there are many indications that Luke
intervened at a number of other places in this story, though to
what extent is a matter of controversy among scholars. We shall
therefore leave the question on one side. The point which is
important for our purpose is clear enough in any case.

We have already established that the finding of the empty tomb
was not enough to generate belief. In our story this point is
underlined, for the Emmaus disciples tell their still unknown
companion that they and their friends were astonished over the
news brought by the women, that some of them (*sic*) had even been
to the tomb, but that they had not seen Jesus. All this had left them
at a loss, as they admit, in spite of the angel's assurance that Jesus
was alive (24.22-24). By the end of the story there has been a complete reversal of situation. Conviction has been achieved: Jesus
lives. But this conviction has been produced through the seeing
of Jesus.

When one has recognized this, another point presently becomes
noticeable. Conviction does not imply that *all* the disciples have
already seen Jesus. For although the eleven and the others who
were with them only knew about the appearance to Peter, they *all*
say: 'The Lord has risen indeed.' The word of an angel was not
enough to produce this conviction. The Emmaus disciples only
have a chance to tell of their encounter with Jesus later. The others
therefore only knew about the appearance to Simon and based their
belief that Jesus was alive on that alone.

We shall pursue this point later. For the moment let us continue
with our examination of the Lucan text. Various scenes now follow
in close succession (24.36-49). While they were talking (that is to
say, late in the evening of the first day of the week and still in

Jerusalem) Jesus appeared among them. They were startled and frightened, supposing that what they saw was a ghost.

One is surprised at this, for in fact the disciples ought now surely to have been prepared. (We remember a similar feature at the close of Matthew's Gospel: although the eleven have been sent to Galilee and have been promised an encounter with the risen Jesus, it is said that some of them doubted.) Jesus now asks why the disciples are so startled (or troubled, according to the RSV). He shows them his hands and his feet and tells them to touch him, pointing out that a spirit has neither flesh nor bones. The reaction of the disciples is a twofold one. On the one hand they are overjoyed; on the other they still do not believe and are astonished. For the second time we ask ourselves how this fits in with the belief attested in 24.34. Jesus now asks whether they have anything to eat. They give him broiled fish and he eats it in their presence. We are not told what the reaction of the disciples was, but they are now apparently convinced.

The teaching of Jesus which follows is in certain respects similar to that given to the disciples on the road to Emmaus. It closes with a missionary charge: repentance and the forgiveness of sins is to be preached in the name of Christ among all peoples, beginning at Jerusalem. The disciples are to be witnesses and Jesus promises them the gift of power from on high. Until then they are to stay in Jerusalem.

I think that two things are clear here. On the one hand much is reminiscent of the end of Matthew's Gospel. The appearance to the disciples leads on to the missionary charge (though in Luke this is given in Jerusalem and in Matthew on the mountain in Galilee). The reason for the disciples' doubt is in both cases curious, for the appearance (in our present account) does not find the disciples unprepared. It must also be said that the idea of the resurrection body is here conceived of in highly material terms. The identity *motif* (the displaying of the hands and feet) is extended to touch – at least this is offered; we are not told whether the offer is taken up – and finally Jesus eats in front of the disciples. Although in places Luke gives the impression of playing down the significance of the empty tomb (it does not produce belief), it must be stressed that his motive is evidently not a 'spiritualization' of the concept. It is true that the appearance of Jesus can seem like the appearance of a spirit; but the essential difference is demonstrated in the most emphatic terms.

The last verses of the Gospel (24.50-53) present us with a multiplicity of problems. It is still the same first day of the week as before; and let us remind ourselves of all that has happened (beginning with the two-hour journey from Emmaus to Jerusalem) since the Emmaus disciples invited Jesus to stay with them because it was evening and the day was far spent. Jesus now leads the disciples out to Bethany. There he lifts up his hands and blesses them and then departs from them. Some manuscripts, though not all, add the sentence 'and was carried up into heaven'. The disciples return to Jerusalem with great joy and are continually to be found in the temple praising God.

Whether the mention of the ascension derives from Luke or is a later addition is again disputed. But there can be no doubt that it is a scene of departure that is being described. The next thing to be expected is power from on high. How does this fit in with the beginning of Luke's sequel, the Acts of the Apostles? There the ascension of Jesus is described as a separate event; but it only takes place forty days after Easter. Numerous attempts have been made to find a solution to the questions which arise here. I cannot go into all the possible answers; nor do they play a particularly important part in connection with our present theme.

In conclusion it may be said that in Luke (more than in Matthew) the Easter happening appears as a series of events. It is true that the details of the narrative are not always consistent. (How many people were at the empty tomb? Why the doubt, since belief has already been affirmed?) Yet the account moves purposefully towards its goal, leading up to the ascension with the sending of the Spirit which follows. And this Spirit, as the spirit of Jesus, then continues his earthly ministry in the Acts of the Apostles. The resurrection is a transitional stage which is conceived of in highly material terms.

(d) The Gospel of John

There is almost universal agreement nowadays that the Fourth Gospel is the latest of the New Testament Gospels and was written in the last decade of the 1st century. Its authorship is disputed. At no point does the Gospel itself claim to have been written by John the apostle. It is only in 21.24 that the author is described as being the disciple whom Jesus loved. But we shall see later that ch. 21 is a later addition appended to chs. 1-20. Moreover, nowhere in the Gospel (not even in ch. 21) is the beloved disciple identified with John.

Now the authorship question could have a certain importance in that one expects greater reliability from an eyewitness account. But there is no doubt (again, nearly all scholars agree here) that the author of this work intervened in the presentation of the narrative to a degree which has no parallel among the other evangelists. This means, however, that the author was not intending to give an accurate report but meant to use his narrative in order to make theological statements. And this reduces the authorship question to one of secondary importance, since the author, whether he was an eyewitness or not, is not concerned with historical accuracy. Incidentally (and it seems to me that this is a point worth mentioning) if one wanted to maintain the historical accuracy of the Fourth Gospel, one would have to deny the accuracy of the other three; for the differences are considerable.

I do not want to spend too much time on preliminary questions and will rather turn at once to the text. But since one must not arbitrarily detach the close from the rest of the work, before we can consider the final section we must know how the author proceeds in the rest of his work; for we are dealing with a largely independent treatment of the material. From now on I shall call the author John, although the question of who the writer actually was must be left open.

The fourth evangelist almost certainly did not know any of the other three Gospels. But since he must have known traditions which were also incorporated into the other works, we shall draw various comparisons in our discussion of the content of his Gospel. He seems to have been particularly close to the traditions which Luke took over.

According to John's Gospel, there stood beneath the cross Jesus' mother, her sister, another Mary (the wife of Clopas) and Mary Magdalene, as well as the beloved disciple (19.25f.). Some of the names are therefore again different, and so is the place, inasmuch as the bystanders are here standing directly beside the cross. Jesus can even speak to them.

After Jesus' death, we are told that his side was pierced with a spear (19.34) and that blood and water flowed from the wound. No other Gospel mentions this. John reverts to this incident later. He does not mention that any of the women were present at the burial, in this differing from all the other Gospels (19.38-42). But in addition to Joseph of Arimathea, Nicodemus (who has already been mentioned in 3.1) is named. John therefore shows a distinct interest in linking up the story with what has gone before. We are then told that the body of Jesus was anointed before burial. Apparently the anointing *motif* has shifted. Mark and Luke could never have said that the women wanted to anoint Jesus *after* his burial if they had supposed that he had been anointed before.

All the stories contained in ch. 20 take place on the first day of the week, with the exception of the story about Thomas. Mary Magdalene comes alone to the tomb (20.1). We are not told why she came, but since in the Johannine context it cannot have been to anoint the body, we must suppose that she wanted to visit the tomb – as in Matthew's version, where the motive is specifically stated.

We now come up against a difficulty. Mary Magdalene finds the stone (which John has not previously mentioned) rolled away from the tomb. This is at first simply stated, no more.

Mary then runs away from the tomb, finds Simon Peter and the beloved disciple and says: 'They have taken the Lord out of the tomb and we (*sic*) do not know where they have laid him'. One asks oneself how Mary Magdalene knew this, since up to then she had merely seen that the stone had been rolled away. It might be replied that although we are not told that she looked in, this is implicit; there is a similar incident in Matthew. But it is noticeable that after the disciples' race to the tomb (20.3-10) – which I shall come back to in a moment – we are told that Mary stood weeping outside (20.11). It was only then that she looked into the tomb and saw two angels clothed in white, who spoke to her. Since we are not told that she had returned to the grave from Peter and the other disciple (to whom she had run after she had discovered that the stone had been rolled away, 20.2), it must be assumed – and modern scholars are here for the most part agreed – that the evangelist inserted the story of the disciples' race into a story about Mary Magdalene's visit to the tomb. And in fact 20.11 can be read as a direct sequel to 20.1. In 20.1 Mary Magdalene comes to the tomb and sees that the stone has been rolled away; in 20.11 she stands at the tomb weeping (for grief, not because she has already missed the body), looks into the tomb and sees two angels.

With this the evangelist's method of procedure becomes clear and probably also what he wanted to convey. A visit to the tomb by certain women was known to him from tradition – which tradition we do not know. John reduces the number to one. (This is probably connected with 20.16.) Mary has the experience with the two angels (in Mark a young man; in Matthew an angel; in Luke two men). The stories of the empty tomb in all the gospels therefore obviously belong to one part of the tradition; and the story of the disciples' race to the tomb belongs to a totally different one. But why is it inserted at this particular point? Why is the story about Mary Magdalene not brought to an end first and the disciples' race described afterwards? This order of events would be entirely comprehensible and would be similar to that in Matthew. There the women find the tomb empty; Jesus then appears to them; and afterwards they find the disciples and send them to Galilee. John could have told his story similarly: Mary Magdalene finds the tomb and the angel, then meets Jesus and afterwards tells Peter and the other disciple. But John presents a different order of events. Why?

I think that we can find an answer to this question. For something has happened here which is very similar to what occurred in

Luke's story of the road to Emmaus, even though that is presented quite differently. In Luke 24.34 the disciples in Jerusalem take the words out of the mouths of the Emmaus disciples, telling of Jesus' appearance to Peter. The priority of this appearance is thus stressed – or preserved. Peter is the first Easter witness. John now first only describes how Mary Magdalene found that the stone had been rolled away. She tells Peter and the other disciple. These run to the tomb. The other disciple arrives first, looks in and sees that the linen grave-clothes are lying neatly rolled together (cf. Luke 24.12 and what was said above); but he does not go into the tomb, allowing Peter the precedence. Peter also sees the grave-clothes rolled together (cf. again Luke 24.12) as well as the napkin which had been round his head, rolled up in another place. Only then does the other disciple enter the tomb – and now we are told 'And he saw and believed' (20.8).

It is not quite clear what is meant here, since the following verse seems contradictory. It runs: 'For as yet they did not know the scripture, that he must rise from the dead' (20.9). This appears to contradict the preceding verse. It has therefore sometimes been assumed that this verse, like ch. 21, belongs to a later editing of John's Gospel, especially since the text reads perfectly smoothly if one follows 20.8 immediately by 20.10. But this question, like many another, must be left open.

One thing may be said with some degree of certainty, however. According to John's Gospel, the sight of the empty tomb does lead to belief, at least in the case of the other disciple. We are told that 'he saw and believed' (20.8). In Luke this was far from the case. It was the angel's reminder of what Jesus had said earlier that convinced the women, not the empty tomb. In John, on the contrary, the mere sight of the empty tomb leads to belief. This is only expressly stated of the 'other' disciple, but we are certainly intended to suppose that Peter (who, according to the account, was first inside the tomb) also believed.

This story of the disciples' race, then, is undoubtedly designed to bring out the priority of Peter in some form or other; and since its point is belief evoked by the empty tomb, one can say that the priority of Peter's faith in the risen Jesus is to be established. Hence the story of Mary Magdalene at the tomb cannot be immediately told to the end, but has to be interrupted. The passage has been edited so as to stress the priority of Peter. The editing looks different from that in Luke (24.34). But may one not suppose that the intention is the same in both cases? In John this is brought out by the immediate mention of the disciple who was the second to believe: the other disciple, whom Jesus loved.

We can now immediately go on to say something else. The scene of the disciples' race was probably the work of the evangelist himself. Among the many reasons which give credence to this theory, three may be mentioned. First there is the figure of the beloved disciple, who is only to be met with in John's Gospel, where he has a particular function, though what this is is a matter of dispute among scholars. Then one must note the 'rivalry' between this disciple and Peter, which is mentioned again twice in ch. 21 and which very probably reflects rivalries in the primitive church. Finally, the older tradition (with the admittedly controversial exception of Luke 24.12) knows only of women at the tomb and nothing of Peter. The evangelist's interpolation makes Peter the first and the other disciple the second who is brought to believe in the risen Jesus.

The writer is then able to finish the story of Mary Magdalene (20.11-18). After Peter and the other disciple have gone home, Mary stands at the tomb weeping. She looks in and sees two angels in white sitting there, at a place which is exactly described: one where Jesus' head and one where his feet had lain. They speak to Mary. 'Woman, why are you weeping?' She answers, 'Because they have taken away my Lord, and I do not know (cf. 20.2: we do not know) where they have laid him.' Oddly, the angels then say nothing more. Mary turns round and sees Jesus but without recognizing him (a *motif* similar to that in the story of the road to Emmaus). Like the angel, Jesus asks why Mary is weeping and adds: 'Whom do you seek?' She takes him to be the gardener and asks directly: 'Sir, if you have carried him away, tell me where you have laid him, and I will take him away.' It is noticeable that the taking away of the body is mentioned for the third time here (20.15; cf. 20.2 and 20.13).

One is bound to ask whether this repetition is a chance one or whether there is a connection with the apologetic *motif* in Matthew. The defence would then, it is true, be in different terms from those of the story of the guard at the tomb. But John's emphasis on the fact that the grave-clothes were folded in orderly fashion (20.5 and 6) and that the napkin was rolled up (20.7) may belong to this motif. For if the body had been stolen this would hardly have been the case. A defence of the empty tomb therefore seems to be behind the story – a defence which was necessary because of the claim that the body of Jesus had been stolen. The defence is not explicit, however; and one cannot therefore be sure that it is intended.

Jesus now speaks to Mary, calling her by her name. She then recognizes him, addressing him as Rabboni. (The Emmaus disciples recognized Jesus at the meal. It is always Jesus who sparks off the recognition.) Then follows a puzzling remark. Jesus says (I quote here from the Authorized Version): 'Touch me not: for I am not yet ascended to my Father: but go to my brethren, and say unto them, I ascend unto my Father, and your Father; and to my God, and your God.'

This remark is not without importance for our theme. For we are enquiring into the concept of the resurrection; and here the question of the tangibility of the risen Jesus could be significant. But how is the passage to be interpreted? Why is Mary not to touch Jesus? One might answer, because one cannot touch a risen body. But to this it might be objected that this is not only possible according to Luke's account but that in the story of Thomas which follows in this very same Gospel, Jesus even invites the disciple to touch him. It is admittedly still conceivable that our present story embodies a tradition in which the tangibility of the resurrection body was denied. In this case the evangelist would simply have failed to reconcile the two viewpoints.

But we must notice the context of the sentence. The injunction 'touch me not' is explained in this translation as being necessary because Jesus has not yet ascended to his Father. But then one must ask whether touch is thought of as being possible later. This is hardly conceivable, for how could one imagine it? But it is equally impossible to say that Jesus ascended to the Father after the meeting with Mary and was then touchable at the later encounters. I believe myself that one should start from the idea that wherever the empty tomb is mentioned the risen Jesus is to be thought of as being tangible.

Various attempts have been made to translate the μή μου ἅπτου more freely as 'Do not hold me back' (cf. RSV 'Do not hold me'). But does this make sense? If the reason for not holding Jesus back is supposed to be that he has not yet ascended to the Father, he must be expected to ascend in the very near future. But this is not the case (at least not in this Gospel). The difficulties disappear if one translates the passage more or less as follows: 'Touch me not, *although* I am not yet ascended to my Father (i.e., you could still touch me, but at this particular moment I want you to do something else, that is:) go to my brethren and say to them . . .' This paraphrase makes sense of the passage. The idea is then that Jesus is tangible *until* he ascends to the Father.

Mary takes no leave of Jesus nor he of her. She immediately follows his command, finds the disciples and tells them that she has seen the Lord and what he said to her (20.18).

Jesus' appearance to the disciples follows, on the evening of the same first day of the week (20.19-23). The disciples (no number is given) are assembled in a room in Jerusalem behind closed doors. Jesus comes (through these closed doors) into the room. He greets the disciples and shows them his hands and his side (not, as in Luke 24.39, his hands and his feet). We are definitely told that the disciples were glad. (In Luke 24.37 they were afraid and first thought that Jesus was a spirit.) In John the doubt *motif* is missing, although it crops up later as the theme of the Thomas story. After another greeting the missionary charge follows, in typically Johannine terminology: 'As the Father has sent me, even so I send you.' Then Jesus breathes on them, giving them the Holy Spirit. In the Fourth Gospel, therefore, Easter and Whitsun really fall on the same day. With the conferring of the Spirit is associated the power to remit and retain sins – a *motif* which meets us in very similar form in Matt. 16.19 and Matt. 18.18, as authority given to Peter in the first passage and to the church in the second; in both cases the authority is the gift of the earthly Jesus. What Jesus here says to the disciples (according to John) is therefore directed both outwards (mission) and inwards (forgiveness of sins).

The similarity of John 20.19-23 to the corresponding passage in Luke (24.36-49) is unmistakable. One must of course also take note of the differences; apart from those already mentioned, Jesus comes through closed doors, is not touched and does not eat in the presence of the disciples. But that this shows a special view of the resurrection body can hardly – in the framework of the gospel account as a whole – be maintained, for the story of Thomas which follows (20.24-29) shows that Jesus *could* be touched.

Here the doubt *motif* forms the actual theme. Thomas, one of the twelve, was not present in Jerusalem on the evening of the first day of the week. He is told the news, but he does not believe. He wants to test the matter for himself and is not prepared to believe until he sees the marks of the nails in Jesus' hands, can put his fingers into these nail marks and his hand into Jesus' side. A week later Jesus again comes through closed doors and challenges Thomas to do exactly what he had demanded as a precondition for his belief. We are not told that Thomas accepts Jesus' challenge, but he confesses: 'My Lord and my God.' The point of the story lies in Jesus' final words: 'Have you believed because you have seen me? Blessed are those who have not seen and yet believe.' But this means that though it had once been possible to see Jesus, now there was only the gospel. Thomas ought to have believed that without demanding any additional guarantee. Although this guarantee has been offered, as an exceptional concession, the normal procedure ought none the less to be faith as a response to the hearing of the message. To formulate this in modern terms: according to John's Gospel one ought to listen to the *kerygma* without insisting on factual evidence. Of course this does not mean that there are no facts behind the *kerygma*. But faith does not first ask for facts before it is prepared to believe. This problem will concern us again later.

John's Gospel originally finished after the Thomas story, 20.30-31 clearly being the book's concluding words. In spite of this the story continues. But the appendix (ch. 21) is very different in kind from the second close of Mark's Gospel (16.9-20). There we are simply dealing with a harmonization of *motifs* from the other Gospels. But John 21 embodies an independent tradition and we must look at it in more detail. I ought perhaps to point out here that scholars are largely agreed that John 21 is not written by the same author as the rest of the Gospel.

The scene changes. What follows no longer takes place in Jerusalem but at the Sea of Tiberias, that is, in Galilee. Up to now the only appearance in Galilee has been at the end of Matthew's Gospel. But that is hardly comparable with the present passage.

The story we are told here is on the whole a strange one. It is an appendix but it explicitly purports to describe a later event. 21.1 is clearly an editorial transition: 'After this Jesus revealed himself again to the disciples by the Sea of Tiberias; and he revealed himself in this way . . .' From 21.2 an earlier tradition is taken over and adapted.

Simon Peter, Thomas, Nathaniel, the sons of Zebedee and two other disciples are all together. Peter proposes to go fishing and the others are going to accompany him. They put out in the boat but catch nothing all night.

If the story is viewed as a continuation of the narrative in ch. 20, it now takes a somewhat surprising turn. Had the disciples not received the missionary charge from Jesus? He had surely sent them forth? But now there is not a word to suggest that they had drawn any practical conclusions from this fact. Nor does the sequel suggest that the disciples had already seen Jesus in Jerusalem. The whole scene has the effect of a first appearance – more: of an *utterly surprising* first appearance. One can best crystallize the impression made by the story if one imagines that the crucifixion has taken place, that the disciples have returned to Galilee – and now they experience the event which forms the substance of this chapter, as a complete surprise and without any preparation (as for example, through the finding of the empty tomb).

Let us follow the story. In the morning, after their lack of success, the disciples bring their boat to shore. There stands Jesus, but (like the Emmaus disciples and Mary Magdalene) the disciples do not recognize him. Jesus asks if they have any fish (AV: if they have anything to eat). They answer 'No'. Jesus then tells them to let down the net on the right side of the boat. They do so and catch so many fish that they are not able to haul the net in. The beloved disciple then says to Peter, 'It is the Lord.' Upon this, Peter pulls on his coat and jumps into the water. The idea, of course, is that he wanted to reach Jesus without loss of time; we are not told, however, whether he succeeds. The other disciples bring the boat to land, where they see a charcoal fire, with fish and bread on it. Food has therefore been prepared. Jesus now tells the disciples to bring some of the fish that they have caught. Peter hauls the net ashore. There are one hundred and fifty-three fish in it, but in spite of this the net does not break. Jesus then invites them to come and eat with him. No one dares to ask who he is, but they know that it is the Lord.

In what is undoubtedly an editorial interpolation, the text adds that this was the third time that Jesus had revealed himself to his disciples (21.14). A motif of particular interest is one which we have already met in connection with the disciples' race to the tomb. Jesus is first recognized by the beloved disciple but Peter is the first who starts out to him. Now it is certainly not expressly stated that Peter is the first actually to reach Jesus (just as it is not expressly stated in 20.6f that Peter believed). One sees that Peter's priority is not disputed but that it is clearly being pushed into the background. The disciple whom Jesus loved moves into the foreground in his stead.

It is this very *motif* which plays a part in what follows (21.15-23). After the meal, Jesus asks Simon Peter: 'Do you love me?' Peter answers, 'Yes, Lord', and receives the command from Jesus, 'Feed my lambs.' The exchange is repeated twice. One is bound to ask whether a (renewed?) missionary charge is being given here. Then Jesus turns to Peter with the words: 'When you were young, you girded yourself and walked where you would; but when you are old, you will stretch out your hands, and another will gird you and carry you where you do not wish to go.' If one does not read on, one is inclined to interpret this in the sense that Peter is now to be *entirely* absorbed in service; it is no longer his will that is important but the will of his Lord. The narrator, however, has a different interpretation, for he adds that Jesus was thus pointing to Peter's martyrdom (21.19). Afterwards Jesus himself speaks to Peter again, saying 'Follow me'; and now Peter turns to the beloved disciple and asks what was to happen to him. The answer is a riddle: 'If it is my will that he remain until I come, what is that to you? Follow me!' Again the narrator comments that the saying then spread among the brethren that this disciple would not die. (This must evidently have been the general opinion originally, although it was later proved erroneous – perhaps by the disciple's death. Would it be too much to suppose that the death of the disciple took place between the date when the Gospel was written and the date of the supplementary chapter?) At all events, the view that Jesus intended to say that the disciple would not die is now rejected as false, and Jesus' saying to Peter is repeated, although this remains a riddle. Then the disciple is claimed to be a true witness. And finally a new closing passage follows (21.24-25).

Chapter 21 naturally raises a multiplicity of questions, questions to which scholars have given very different answers, as may be imagined. In particular, attempts have repeatedly been made to explain the curious parallelism of Peter and the other disciple. But in whatever direction we may hope to find an answer, one thing can be said with certainty: the parallelism is typically Johannine. The beloved disciple only appears in the Fourth Gospel. We meet him three times together with Peter: at the race to the tomb; in the boat on the sea of Tiberias; and at the missionary charge. Here, therefore, the evangelist (20.2-10) and the author of ch. 21 have intervened in the tradition. If the results of this intervention are carefully peeled away, remains of an older tradition come to light in ch. 21: Jesus' unexpected appearance to Peter while he is fishing in Galilee, and the command to Peter no longer to work in his own name but in the name of another.

Let us leave this on one side for the present. Now that we have examined the texts of the Gospels, we can take up the theme of our discussion once more.

4. Conclusions and Continuing Questions

Let us call to mind our original question. We wanted information or, to be more precise, we wanted to discover the concepts that prompted the evangelists when they made their statement of faith 'Jesus is risen'.

First of all, it must be pointed out that at no point is the resurrection itself within our field of vision. Here tradition is at one. We are nowhere told that anyone witnessed the resurrection of Jesus, nor is the resurrection itself described. In every case we have to do with encounters with Jesus after his death. These naturally presuppose that something has happened between the crucifixion and the encounters; but *what* has happened remains shrouded in mystery. The event is never described or related.

We call what happened resurrection. But what does this mean? That is what we wanted to try to find out. But we cannot discover the answer – or at least not directly. The only possible way of approaching the matter more closely is to start from the encounters and to trace back, asking, roughly speaking, what *must* have happened to make these meetings possible?

But here we are faced with the difficulty that we have very different descriptions of the meetings. The results seem confusing, as we have seen. Can they somehow or other be so ordered as to produce an acceptable result?

There is a certain amount of common ground. All the way through, the concepts are highly 'material'. This can be demonstrated from two features in particular: the empty tomb; and the fact that Jesus could be touched and that he ate with or in front of his disciples. It is almost as if the dead Jesus had returned to life in his old body. It could probably be said with some degree of certainty that this was at least the way in which the evangelists conceived the resurrection; at all events they would so have answered if they had been asked.

Yet this impression is contradicted by other features. Although there is identity, Jesus is not necessarily recognizable (cf. the Emmaus disciples, Mary Magdalene, the fishermen on the Sea of Tiberias). Here the eyes of the witnesses have always to be opened first; and so we are bound to ask – why was this necessary if Jesus appeared in his old body?

Moreover we meet with the same *motif* in another form. The identity is not merely established after a certain time; it is demonstrated visually. Jesus shows the marks of his wounds (in Luke his hands and feet, in John his hands and side). The point that is brought out here is that the one whom the disciples saw is identical with the crucified. But again the question is – why does the identity have to be expressly demonstrated?

Finally, one must also point in this connection to the doubts of the witnesses. We hear of these at the end of Matthew's Gospel as well as in Luke, where the doubt has to be demolished step by step when Jesus appears to the assembled disciples in Jerusalem. Finally, in John's Gospel the motif is thematically developed in the story of Thomas.

Thus although the stories always have to do with the Jesus who has returned from the grave, his identity is not immediately ascertainable. It is either recognizable after 'their eyes were opened'; or it has to be expressly stressed; or the doubt has to be overcome. Formulated as question and answer the problem might be stated as follows: 'Is it really *he* whom they have seen?' 'Yes, it is *he*.'

There is another set of problems as well. The 'body' of Jesus is conceived of in different terms at the different appearances. On the one hand we have the 'material' features (the tomb was empty; Jesus eats; he can be touched), on the other, Jesus can pass through closed doors. The two are not easily reconcilable. And in this connection we must ask ourselves where the evangelist thought the risen Jesus actually was. Only Luke is consistent here, speaking of the ascension, at least in the Acts of the Apostles. (As we have seen, Luke 24.51 presents textual difficulties. But all the same it is clearly a scene of departure that is described.) In Mark we learn nothing (which could, however, be explained by the mutilated ending).

Matthew and John are silent on the subject. We are of course easily inclined to read Luke's close into the other Gospels. But here one must be cautious. Why do they not mention it? If one is *interested* in the risen body of Jesus, if it is important to convey an accurate idea of it, then one surely cannot silently pass the problem by? This argument has all the more force since we must not simply project our knowledge of all the Gospels into the early church, presupposing that all four were known there. Matthew, for example, intended to give a complete account. He did not expect his readers to learn from Luke that Jesus had ascended into heaven. If Matthew had known anything about the ascension, he would certainly have told what he knew at the end of the scene on the mountain in Galilee. But how could he have failed to know about it? And why does he not seem to feel the need even to touch on the whereabouts of the risen Jesus? We are in fact given an answer: the risen Lord remains with his disciples until the end of the world – but hardly, surely, in the same body in which he has earlier been presented as having risen.

All this forces one ultimately to ask whether the question which interests us today (the resurrection body of Jesus) was simply of no interest at all at the time? For this is what the picture's lack of unity would suggest.

But we did not, after all, merely want to enquire into the concepts which were used by the witnesses who tell of Jesus' resurrection; we also wanted to find out whether, in confessing today that 'Jesus is risen', we are bound to think of the word 'risen' in a particular conceptual framework, and can only truly make the confession of faith in this one sense. For, as I mentioned at the beginning of these lectures, that is what is maintained today; and this is what was once again stated in the Düsseldorf Declaration of the 'Confessional Movement' on Repentance Day 1967. (I shall look briefly at this Declaration in a moment.)

Paul is often appealed to in this particular difficulty. Does he really take us any further? It is true that in I Cor. 15 Paul, though saying nothing about the nature of the risen body of Jesus, does speak of the body in which the dead will be raised. And since, in I Cor. 15.20,

Paul then speaks of Christ as being the 'first fruits' of the resurrection, it is perhaps permissible to deduce something about the body in which Jesus *was* raised from the bodies in which the dead *are to be raised*. This has frequently been done, the term which Paul uses being taken to explain the closing passages of the Gospels – where, however, the term never occurs! Paul speaks of a 'spiritual' body in which the dead are raised and into which those who are still alive at the second coming of Christ will be changed. This seems to offer a solution. Since Jesus was raised in a spiritual body, he was not immediately recognizable and could pass through closed doors.

But this solution is in fact useless. A term used by Paul, and by Paul alone, cannot be taken out of its context and transferred to the Gospel accounts. We must at least first clarify what Paul understood under the term 'spiritual body'. For this we must read I Cor. 15.35-55 as a whole. Here I can only touch on one or two points.

First, it is important to realize that this chapter is a polemic. There are people in Corinth who deny the resurrection of the dead. They apparently do so on highly rational grounds: the body decays in the ground. In what body can a person then be raised? To this Paul answers: in a spiritual body.

At this point a difficulty arises over the translation. This is connected with the fact that here two basically different anthropologies come up against one another. Paul speaks of $\sigma\hat{\omega}_{,,}\alpha$, a word generally translated as 'body'. When *we* use the word body, we generally understand by it the flesh which decays in the earth. But Paul uses $\sigma\omega\mu\alpha$ to mean identity of the personality before and after death. Those who rise are the same as those who were alive. It is the same 'I', as it were.

Now when Paul speaks of the earthly body (it would be better to translate it as the earthly 'I'), then this earthly 'I' can be seen and touched and can eat and drink; it is 'flesh and blood'. The risen 'I' (that is, the spiritual body) exists in a form which is completely separated from this mode of existence. What this body (this 'I') looks like, Paul is, in the nature of things, unable to say; nor does he attempt to do so. He merely maintains (with the help of the term 'body') the identity of the 'I' – though its mode of existence is totally different.

What is now of interest to us is the way in which the transition is conceived. Paul compares the earthly body (that is, the 'I' existing in flesh and blood) with a grain of corn which is sown, dies and decays. The spiritual body (that is, the 'I' in a completely different and inconceivable mode of existence) does not, however, presuppose that flesh and blood, the body which was laid in the earth, is filled with new life. At this point Paul admits the validity of the Corinthian objection: the body mortifies – and a spiritual body does not therefore presuppose an empty grave. What is laid in the grave is according to Paul precisely *not* the body (or 'I') which is *going to be*; it is the passing, perishable and corruptible body (cf. v. 42). The spiritual body (the risen 'I') is hence not something like an ethereal body (that is, a body minus the earthly conditions), where the earthly corporeality is still visible but the earthly substance is missing.

With the term 'spiritual body' the identity of the earthly 'I' is maintained; but the spiritual body eludes the imagination. Paul can only express what he means through images and analogies. But this shows that we cannot simply tear out of its context a term which occurs in Paul and trim it to an idea of our own, which then seems to fit into a completely different context. For it just will not fit! This is no way out of the difficulty. Here the empty tomb would even be an inconvenience. And of course a spiritual body in the Pauline sense cannot eat or be touched.

Let us now gather up the threads once more. We asked whether we can draw any conclusions about the resurrection itself from the way in which the evangelists depict the resurrection body. This proved to be impossible because of the variation in the accounts. Now we must be clear about the fact that the form of our question derived from the point which is a matter of controversy today. That is to say, we have approached the texts with our special interests in mind. But the texts have no answer – or at least no direct answer – to give to our particular questions. No order can be found in the confusing evidence from this angle. Of course we cannot forget our question, but we must first lay it on one side and ask instead whether there is another approach to the confusing impressions of the texts which might bring order into the confusion (or seeming confusion, as I should already like to stress). In my opinion such an approach can in fact be found.

In spite of all differences in detail there is also common ground. Let us start from that. It consists in the fact that all the evangelists represent the Easter happening as a sequence of events. However differently these may be depicted in detail, it is always a sequence; and I have several times pointed out the links which have been deliberately introduced, for example in the case of the women's names, in the story of the guard at the tomb, etc.

Now we came across a sequence earlier, in the Apostles' Creed – a sequence reviewing the whole of the path which Jesus took. *One* stage of this progress was: 'The third day he rose again from the dead.' This one stage now appears in the Gospels as a differentiated series, as a course of events.

We must of course put this more precisely. The Apostles' Creed is later than the Gospels. The Gospels describe a sequence of events. The Apostles' Creed does not actually summarize these events – it names *the* event which *precedes* the sequence in the Gospels – an event which is not itself described there: the third day he rose again.

But in determining that the Gospels depict the Easter events as a sequence, we must distinguish between two different things. It is one thing to say that the evangelists depicted the Easter event as a sequence (of course in the conviction that this sequence was the correct one). It is another matter to assert that they in fact depicted the sequence as it actually happened. Here a distinction must be made. A person's opinion about an event need not necessarily tally with the event itself.

Let me ask once again: is it only a sceptic who can make such a distinction? Surely not, for our texts positively force the distinction upon us. It is only avoidable if one starts from a hypothesis which has, indeed, been frequently adopted. According to this, the individual evangelists did not describe the whole of the Easter happening, but only a part of it. They selected. If we want to discover the actual course of events we must synthesize and arrange the material.

This hypothesis proves completely untenable, however, if we are prepared to take the texts as they stand. None the less we shall look at the theory briefly. We shall then discover why it is untenable; but in the process we shall come upon a clue which we can then pursue further.

At the beginning always stands the story of the empty tomb. I will not go into the different accounts for the moment. We have already seen that Matthew and Luke are dependent on Mark, but that the Johannine tradition (with Mary Magdalene) also has a certain connection with the tradition found in Mark. If the aim were a harmonization, the empty tomb could be said to be the first event in the sequence. Even if later narrators have modified the account (and so no longer present a correct course of events, at least as regards the details) we still have in Mark, at least, the original tradition. But even if something like a harmonization can if necessary be achieved here, insurmountable difficulties begin with the attempt at reconstructing the later course of events.

Most noticeable of all are, first, the differences as regards the places mentioned. Anyone who is aiming at a harmonization must of course make the happenings in and around Jerusalem precede those in Galilee. Then roughly the following series would emerge:

1. The appearances of Jesus to the two women at the tomb (in Matthew; in John to Mary Magdalene only). This is contradicted by Luke, not merely by the way but quite specifically; in fact he contradicts it in two different ways.

(a) The disciples on the road to Emmaus tell their still unknown companion that women had found the tomb empty and that angels had appeared to them; that other disciples had then seen the empty tomb but that *no one had seen Jesus* (24.24). This is as much as to say that the appearance of Jesus would have set their doubts at rest. Thus the appearance to the women at the tomb is expressly denied.

(b) After their return to Jerusalem the story the Emmaus disciples had to tell was anticipated by the cry: 'The Lord is risen indeed and has appeared to Simon', the intention being to assert the priority of the appearance to Peter. This appearance must be considered as having taken place in Jerusalem (though not at the empty tomb). At least it is supposed to have been the first.

There are therefore two rival statements: the first appearance was to the women at the tomb; the first appearance was to Peter.

2. The appearance to the disciples on the road to Emmaus. Only Luke contributes this story; but since we are told that it took place in the late afternoon and evening of Easter Sunday, two hours' journey from Jerusalem, it does not directly clash with the sequence of the other gospels. The writers could have left the story out for some reason or other.

3. The appearance to the disciples in a house in Jerusalem. Both Luke (24.36-49) and John (20.19-23) report this, but their accounts differ greatly, the only common features being the demonstration of identity and the missionary charge. Among the many differences, one of particular importance is the gift of the Spirit in John, which according to Luke only takes place fifty days later. The would-be harmonizer will hardly be inclined to maintain that there were two different appearances. But if there was only one, who reports it correctly? Were the disciples first doubtful (Luke) or were they immediately overjoyed (John)? What were the words with which Jesus sent the disciples forth? Did Jesus breath on them, giving them the gift of the Holy Spirit (John), or not (Luke)?

4. The appearance to Thomas a week later. Only John relates this. The problem, however, is different from that presented by the story of the Emmaus disciples (cf. 2 above), for we are bound to ask why the disciples remained so long in Jerusalem, although (according to Matthew) they were supposed to go to Galilee forthwith. Moreover the meeting in Galilee is evidently held out to the disciples as their *first* sight of Jesus.

5. The appearances in Galilee, i.e.:

(*a*) to the eleven disciples on the mountain in Galilee (end of Matthew's Gospel);

(*b*) to Peter and six other disciples on the occasion of the miraculous draught of fishes (John 21).

Here it would be very difficult to determine the order of events.

In this connection it must be noted in the first place that Luke excludes the appearances in Galilee – again not merely by the way but quite expressly. This is shown by his deviation in 24.6 from Mark 16.7 (the pointing forward to Galilee becomes a *reminiscence* of Galilee), as well as by Jesus' command to the disciples to remain in Jerusalem until Pentecost (Luke 24.49), a command which they then, according to Luke, obey.

But now other difficulties are added. If we read the end of Matthew with an open mind we do not gather the impression that the appearance here described has been preceded by other appearances to the same group in Jerusalem. Moreover we ask ourselves why the missionary charge has to be repeated if it has already been given in Jerusalem (cf. 3 above). The appearance on the occasion of the miraculous draught seems even more curious. The fact that the disciples had already (even according to John himself) received their commission to go out and preach the Gospel has absolutely no influence on the events in John 21. They go about their daily tasks as if nothing had happened.

The conclusion is inescapable: a synchronizing harmony of the different accounts proves to be impossible. Anyone who persists in the attempt must alter the texts and declare the differences to be trivialities.

In this connection I should like to quote briefly one point of the Düsseldorf Declaration of the 'Confessional Movement', already mentioned. It runs as follows:

We must also reject the false doctrine that the New Testament Easter witnesses clothed their message in mythically coloured legends or that they did not intend to report the appearances of the risen Lord (as the basis and presupposition of faith) in the form in which they really occurred.

A number of different ideas are conjoined in this sentence. I shall come back to the problem meant by the words 'mythically coloured legends' in a different connection. It is then stated that the New Testament Easter witnesses (by which are apparently meant not the pre-New Testament witnesses of an event, whose evidence we no longer possess, but – in our case – the evangelists) intended to present the appearances of the risen Jesus as being the basis and presupposition of faith. I believe this to be correct, although this point too must be discussed later. But we run into difficulties when it is called 'false doctrine' to claim that the evangelists did not intend to report the appearances as they really occurred. In order that we may be clear about what is really being said here, let me reverse the sentence. 'True doctrine' would then be: 'The Easter witnesses of the New Testament intended to report the appearances of the risen Jesus (as the basis and presupposition of faith) in the form in which they really occurred.' I shall leave on one side the question of whether one can here usefully speak of a 'doctrine' at all. But I must put the question: how do the authors of the Düsseldorf Declaration know what the intentions of the evangelists were? These can surely only be deduced from the texts. But if one reads the texts carefully (I am afraid that this has not been done) and still maintains that the evangelists wanted to report the appearances as they really occurred, then one must immediately add: 'Of course they did not succeed.' But what does 'true doctrine' then mean? On the one hand one exposes the incompetence of the evangelists, for one is bound to establish that they were apparently incapable of carrying out their intention. And at the same time one throws away any chance of perhaps still arriving at the event which one is trying to reach.

I have more confidence in the achievement of the evangelists than the authors of this declaration. I believe that they achieved what they wanted to do. But what they wanted to do was not what the Düsseldorf Declaration imputes to them. In saying this I am not even denying that the evangelists (very probably) thought that the Easter events happened in the form in which they describe them. But their opinions about these events then obviously diverged. And then it becomes necessary to make the distinction which I have already indicated, namely to differentiate between the conviction that is held about the course of an event and the event itself. But this means that at the time when the evangelists were writing their

Gospels, there was no longer a unified view in the primitive church about the mode of the Easter happening. This does not seem to have played the decisive part then which is often ascribed to it today. For if people had been really interested in the mode of the resurrection, this would surely have been depicted in uniform terms.

But this brings us to the only question that leads any further. If we do not mean to reproach the evangelists with incompetence, we must ask what their achievement really was. Since it is not possible to harmonize the course of events, we must go on to ask, why not? Why were the evangelists *able* to depict events so differently and why did they do so? This question can in fact be answered with certainty; and the answer offers a new opening.

Again we must not consider the end of the Gospels in isolation. For the evangelists did not proceed differently here from elsewhere. Let me remind you once more of the two-source theory. Mark presented Matthew and Luke with their general scheme, but these two introduced individual traditions into this scheme. We definitely know today that the Jesus tradition began with the transmission of individual blocks of tradition. It is well known that this is also true of the Easter traditions. Since Matthew and Luke only knew Mark as far as the story of the empty tomb, no later sequence of events was at their disposal. They created the sequence themselves by joining together what were originally individual units of tradition. In the case of John's Gospel one cannot prove this so directly (except for ch. 21) since we no longer have the original from which he worked. But since here too the Easter story consists of individual elements, one may presuppose that the same thing applies to the Fourth Gospel. It then follows, however, that the order in which the evangelists arranged the individual traditions was their own.

This then leads to a further question: can one recognize any particular themes as determining the evangelists' arrangement of the individual traditions in their works? The following would be conceivable: the evangelists, working from the existing units of tradition, ask themselves in what order the Easter events can have taken place. Since there was no uniform tradition on this point in the primitive church, each evangelist did the best he could to establish the supposedly correct order. This would explain the varying arrangement.

But there is another factor to be taken into consideration as well. We know today with certainty that each of the evangelists was ruled by a particular conception in writing his work. This conception was determined by the period at which he wrote, the readers for whom he was writing and the theological problems with which he had to deal. And it found one of its forms of expression in the ordering of the material throughout the work – including, of course, the final sections. It can be shown, for example, that Luke works out his conception with the help of geographical information, among other things. The Church starts from Jerusalem. Galilee's greatness is a thing of the past. Hence Luke, in contrast to his Marcan source (16.7), leaves out the sending of the disciples to Galilee. Instead he reminds his readers of what Jesus *had earlier proclaimed* in Galilee (24.6). Consequently the Easter events in Luke are localized in and round Jerusalem.

I cannot go into the different conceptions of the four Gospels in detail in our present context. Nor is this necessary for our argument, for in spite of all differences of individual viewpoint, the common ground is clear enough. It is this to which one should direct one's attention first of all. If one does not separate the end from the beginning – if, that is to say, one really sees each work as a whole – one can see that *all the evangelists want to show that the activity of Jesus goes on*. It goes on in spite of his death on the cross; and it remains the activity of the same Jesus who was once active on earth. The conclusions of the different works are therefore designed to explain why what we have been told about the past (with respect to Jesus' words and works) is not a thing of the past at all, but is vitally relevant to the present. In other words, the evangelists want to address their readers – but the address is to remain *the address of Jesus*.

The identity *motif*, which we came across several times in the different Easter stories, now meets us in the unity of the four works, even though its presentation is individual. From the appearance of Jesus down to his present activity there is a continuity.

But if what needs to be said is that the activity of Jesus goes on, then it is really relatively unimportant whether this is stated in a 'historically' correct order or (if the right order is no longer known) in an order which is only supposedly correct. The problem does not lie in the historical details but in the fact itself. Because (unlike other people belonging to the past) Jesus is not dead but alive, what he said and did in the past determines faith *now*. And that is precisely what the endings of the Gospels bring out.

The cause of Jesus goes on beyond Good Friday – in a miraculous way, it must be added. And the fact that it goes on is always due to a new emergence and intervention of Jesus, to a new commission. There are varying ideas about the way in which the sparking off of the new mission is to be conceived. This was evidently not 'dogmatically' defined, to express the matter in modern terms. The mode is obviously not a question of faith.

Again, we must formulate this more precisely. At the time when the evangelists were writing, the mode of the resurrection was not an article of faith and was not part of a universal Christian conviction. It was possible to be convinced of the continuing activity of Jesus without having to express in uniform terms the exact way in which this continuing activity was achieved.

Let us remind ourselves yet again of the question we put at the beginning of these lectures. Is a particular view of the mode of the resurrection an essential ingredient of faith in the risen Jesus? The evangelists answer this question with an unequivocal 'No'. But can one presuppose the same answer for the earlier period, before the Gospels, which were written between about AD 70 and 100? This question forces us to try and penetrate behind the work of the evangelists.

III The Pre-Gospel Tradition

Since the order of the Easter events in the Gospels has now proved to lack primary authority, we are freed from the necessity of abiding by it; and the opportunity is open to us to compare the individual traditions apart from the order in which they occur in the Gospels and apart also from their topographical detail.

One type of appearance story stands out. It might be characterized in general terms as an appearance to the disciples in association with a missionary charge. The number of disciples is not always the same in the accounts. According to Luke it was the eleven and those who were with them (24.36; cf. 24.33); Matthew mentions only the eleven (28.16); John, the disciples in general (20.19). But we are intended in each case to think of the group that had gathered round the earthly Jesus. The details adorning the appearance stories of this type differ as well. The missionary charge is formulated in varying terms. It is easy to show that much in the accounts is characteristic of the particular evangelist who is writing, and that he was therefore exercising a formative influence. But if all this is stripped away, the remaining agreement is all the greater. This means that these three parallel stories apparently derive from one basic source. They belong to the same block of tradition.

The stories of the empty tomb presented us with a similar situation. But there is an important difference. In the four accounts of the empty tomb it was possible to show that those in Matthew and Luke are definitely derived from Mark and that even John's story (Mary Magdalene's visit to the tomb) is a further development which could be explained on the basis of Mark's narrative. Here, therefore, it is possible to discover the earliest form available to us. But this is not so in the case of the appearances to the disciples. It is impossible to establish mutual dependence. We cannot say exactly what the original story was like, although we may make a reasonable conjecture about the elements which were probably included: the appearance to the disciples (possibly with the 'doubt' *motif*), the identity theme and the missionary charge.

With this we have achieved a preliminary order. Detached from their respective contexts, there is *one* story about the empty tomb (that handed down by Mark) and *one* story about the appearance to the disciples. There are also additional appearance stories which have only been passed down once: the Emmaus story; the Thomas story (this probably being Johannine in origin, however) and the miraculous draught on the Sea of Tiberias (heavily revised). The order of the appearances must remain provisionally unsettled. Were the Emmaus disciples the first to see Jesus? Or was it Peter? Or the eleven? Or some of the women? This puts us roughly in the situation of the evangelists. We have individual traditions and are faced with the problem of whether they can be arranged in a sequence.

Now we are in the fortunate position of having a text which can help us, I Cor. 15.3-8 – although we shall not be too hasty in attempting a harmonization of this text with the individual traditions, especially now that we have seen how problematic harmonizations are (I need only remind you of the key-word 'spiritual body'). So let us first look at I Cor. 15 in isolation.

Paul explains the reason for his remarks in v. 12. There are people in Corinth who deny the resurrection of the dead. From this Paul concludes that they therefore also deny the resurrection of Christ (v. 13). In order to refute this opinion, the apostle sets down the Christian tradition at the very beginning of the chapter. He has passed this tradition on to the Corinthians in the form in which he himself received it (v. 3). The terminology used here shows that the formulation is not Paul's own but that he is adopting and passing on traditional material. The passage runs as follows: 'For I delivered to you as of first importance what I also received, that Christ died for our sins in accordance with the scriptures, that he was buried, that he was raised on the third day in accordance with the scriptures, καὶ ὤφθη [and that he appeared or let himself be seen] by Peter, then by the twelve (*sic*). Then he appeared to more than five hundred brethren at one time, most of whom are still alive, though some have fallen asleep. Then he appeared to James, then to all the apostles. Last of all, as to one untimely born, he appeared also to me [Paul].'

Now we must be precise in our formulations here. Paul cites this chain of witnesses in order to point out that they all *proclaim* Jesus' resurrection (v. 11: 'Whether then it was I or they, so we preach and so you believed'). But this means that neither those he names nor he himself were witnesses of the resurrection itself; they were witnesses of the post-resurrection appearances. And this is a distinction which must be preserved. Because it is frequently ignored, let me clarify the point once again. The people mentioned here in the text are often called witnesses of the resurrection, but this designation is only correct if one means by it that they all *proclaim* the resurrection. They did not experience it. Their experience is described as seeing Jesus.

Now this passage presents a multiplicity of problems, some of which are still unsolved. It is a question, for example, where the traditional material taken over by Paul stops and where he himself intervenes in the tradition with new formulations or editorial emendations. What he says about the five hundred brethren does not fit into the formula stylistically, and the reference to the appearance he himself experienced was certainly added by his own hand. It is then noticeable that two distinct groups crystallize out, each of them with a single individual at its head: Peter/the twelve; and James/all the apostles. This raises the question of the relationship of the twelve to the apostles. Are the apostles a wider circle? But Peter belongs both to the twelve and to the apostles. Did he experience three appearances? Paul was also an apostle, but although 'all the apostles' are mentioned, Paul cannot mean to include himself here.

A number of solutions to this question (and others) have been put forward and I shall not go into them now. We shall take as our point of departure what can be established with some degree of certainty. Paul obviously means to say that the appearance to him was the last of the resurrection appearances. And then we can equally well go on to say that in Paul's opinion the first appearance was to Peter. Probably Paul is here listing the appearances in order, since the copulative form used is always: then, then (even though two different words are used in the Greek).

This can take us a stage further if we compare the tradition which we have crystallized out of the Gospels. The order would now be as follows: the first appearance was to Peter; the appearance to the twelve comes afterwards. (It is worth noticing that Paul speaks of the twelve, although according to the Gospels it can only have been eleven.)

Further comparisons are not possible. An appearance to James is not mentioned in any of the Gospels (which were written some twenty to fifty years after Paul), nor do they record an appearance to all the apostles nor one to more than five hundred brethren at once. Were these no longer known about later? Or, if they were known, were they thought to have been later appearances? But then Luke, at least, would surely have mentioned them in the Acts of the Apostles. For the time being we are unable to account for the silence. So we shall content ourselves meanwhile with what we can be more or less sure of: that the first appearance was to Peter and that the appearance to the twelve followed.

Let us now compare this with what the evangelists have to say. Matthew does not mention the appearance to Peter at all. In John it is recorded, though not as the first appearance, but only in the supplementary chapter. Admittedly, on the basis of our previous argument, the order in the Gospels need no longer disturb us. But another point then becomes of interest.

We have established that Luke aims to preserve the priority of the appearance to Peter, the method being to allow the disciples in Jerusalem to anticipate the words of the Emmaus disciples. It is true that the appearance to Peter is not *described*; it is simply mentioned and, moreover, in a form which is reminiscent, even terminologically, of I Cor. 15.5.

Let us remember further that in the disciples' race to the tomb there was a recognizable intention to preserve Peter's priority. Before Jesus appeared to Mary Magdalene and she believed, Peter and the other disciple believed already (though in this case because of the empty tomb).

It was therefore apparently part of the tradition that Peter was the first to believe, although various versions of how he came to do so were passed down: I Cor. 15.5 and Luke 24.34 simply mention an appearance without describing it in detail; John describes how Peter was the first to enter the empty tomb. It is only in John 21 that we have a detailed appearance account. But this is no longer described as being the first appearance (at least in the framework of the Johannine work). Let us remember, however, that when we were considering John 21 we were surprised that, in spite of the missionary charge given to the disciples in Jerusalem, Peter and the others went about their daily tasks in Galilee as if nothing had happened. When once the story is detached from the Gospel framework, it gives the impression of reporting a first appearance.

We are now faced with the question of how the simple statements of the fact that Peter was the first to believe fit in with the detailed account of *how* he came to do so (John 21). In the framework of the Peter tradition this is still obscure. It is hard to find motifs to investigate and compare. We can only make any progress by putting the same question to the other block of tradition, which describes the appearance to the twelve (or to the eleven, or to the disciples). As we have said, there can be hardly a doubt that here we have to do with a tradition which springs from a single root. This tradition has been taken over by Matthew, Luke and John and built into narrative accounts which tell the story in different ways.

The mere mention of this appearance in the formula transmitted by Paul may therefore well be an early form of this particular tradition. It would then run simply: 'and afterwards (he appeared) to the twelve.' The way in which this 'Jesus appeared to the twelve' was interpreted is shown by the Gospel accounts: the appearance to the disciples sparked off their commission. The missionary charge which we meet with everywhere makes this clear. The point of these accounts was not to report *the fact that Jesus appeared* but to explain the reason for making disciples of all nations, baptizing them and teaching them to keep what Jesus had commanded (Matthew); the reason for proclaiming repentance to all nations in the name of Jesus (Luke); the reason for knowing oneself to be sent by Jesus, just as Jesus had been sent by the Father (John). One might paraphrase the statement by saying: 'It is not our own cause which we are pursuing; it is the cause of Jesus which we are *continuing* to pursue; and we are doing this because he appeared to us after his crucifixion and because that has plunged us into faith and mission.'

We must now, however, verify what we have done. We have interpreted *one* section of the formula transmitted by Paul ('he appeared to the twelve') in the light of subsequent tradition. Is this permissible? Is what the later tradition *says* already implicit in this part of the Pauline formula? To put it in oversimplified and alternative terms: is 'he appeared to the twelve' simply and exclusively a report of what the twelve *experienced*? Or is 'he appeared to the twelve' also an explanation of the function which the twelve now have? It is impossible to tell merely from the wording of the formula.

But in fact one ought not to see the two things as alternatives. If the stress lies on the function, the vision is not thereby disputed (as the basis for the exercise of the function). If the stress is on the having seen, however, this does not necessarily exclude a functional consequence.

We have therefore to do with the same problem which I indicated at the beginning of the lectures. The contemporary reference of the credal 'Jesus lives' does not deny the past; the dead Jesus is alive once more. On the other hand even emphasis on the past event intends that what happened should have significance today. The matter only differs from what we said earlier in as much as the problem no longer centres on the resurrection itself but on the 'having seen'. We shall therefore have to clarify the relationship between the seeing and the resurrection. But let us keep to our present theme for the moment.

We have two traditions: one section of the Pauline formula (Jesus appeared to the twelve; here the function is not expressly stated) and the tradition found in the Gospels (where – through the missionary charge – the function is explicitly named). But the question is: may we, or must we, find the function to be at least implicit in this part of the formula? Although we cannot decide this as regards the formula itself, we are not entirely without an answer to the question, for the way in which Paul, at least, *understood* the formula can be shown. Let us remember that the apostle is attacking the opinions of those people in Corinth who denied the resurrection of the dead and thus (Paul adds) were also bound to deny the resurrection of Jesus. As the basis of his argument he names witnesses, stressing that all of them had seen Christ. But he does not close the list of witnesses (as would perhaps have seemed the obvious course) with the observation: 'Since we all saw him, he must have risen; and consequently your doubt in the resurrection of the dead is unfounded.' If Paul had said this he would have been interpreting the 'seeing' of the formula in the sense that it was an isolated focus of interest and thereby vouched for the factual nature of the resurrection. But Paul does not argue quite like that. After he has named himself as the last witness to see Jesus (thereby stressing the extraordinary nature of his 'vision'), he comes directly to the function of that vision: 'I worked harder than any of them' (I Cor. 15.10). The seeing of Jesus led him (and the others) to go to work – i.e., it made them missionaries of the gospel. He then goes on, 'Whether then it was I or they, so we preach and so you believed.'

There can therefore be no doubt that Paul understood the formula (even though it does not explicitly mention a function) as function-*determining*. Admittedly this does not tell us whether the originator of the formula also directly meant to imply the function or whether he merely wanted to bring out the fact that Jesus was seen.

Nothing can be proved. But even before we have established the correct interpretation of the seeing, there is a point which is worth consideration. Let me put forward two alternative possibilities. Did people first see Jesus; then define what they saw; having defined it, reflect on the consequences that must result from seeing; and then, and only then, say: 'seeing constrains us to preach the gospel?' Or were the seeing and the missionary charge one and the same from the very first, so that seeing alone could be named since the function was in any case implicit?

As regards the transmission this would mean the following. In the first case (where one idea follows on another) one must take the formula presented by Paul to be the earliest available starting point of the tradition – a tradition which would then be concentrated unilaterally on the establishment of the seeing. Out of this a tradition would later have evolved which added the mission *motif*; and this tradition would then (after further development) have found its way into the Gospels. In the other case (where seeing and mission are bound up together from the beginning) one must view all the traditions as being further developments of this source. In the form repeated by Paul only the seeing would then be mentioned (for a reason which must still be clarified). In the traditions which have found their way into the final sections of the Gospels we would then have before us further developments of this seminal stage.

Both possibilities are conceivable. I personally think that the second is more probable, but that is no argument. How can we get any further? I think by returning to the Peter traditions and by weighing up what we have observed in the traditions about the disciples.

Let us then first turn to the story told in the chapter appended to the Fourth Gospel. We decided that this gave the impression of being the account of a first appearance. Was this really the case?

Let me try to peel away the editorial accretions. The beloved disciple is certainly one of these. We must eliminate him from the story if we want to approach its original form. But probably the other disciples do not originally belong to the story either, for they are, so to speak, only 'extras'. This is also suggested by a comparison with the other appearance stories. In these the functional aspect (the missionary charge) touches all the people who are present at the appearance. In our story there is also this functional aspect, but it only affects Peter. The other disciples seem to be forgotten. This makes it reasonable to suppose that they were introduced into the story at a later stage.

This functional aspect now meets us in double form. First we have to do with the threefold commission to Peter to feed Jesus' sheep. This presupposes that there is a church to be fed. But is there one yet? One does not necessarily, however, have to think of the church which was gathered together by missionary activity after Easter; the word could certainly refer to the disciples who had drifted away from one another after the crucifixion. Peter is to look after them. Then we have the following saying: 'When you were young, you girded yourself and walked where *you* would; but when you are old, you will stretch out your hands, and another will gird you and carry you where you do *not* wish to go.' In the Gospel itself this saying is interpreted as pointing to Peter's martyrdom. But this interpretation must be a secondary one. What was the original meaning? I believe that here we have something in the nature of a missionary charge. Up to now Peter has acted in his own name; now he is to act in the name of another. One might formulate it as follows (thus immediately bringing out a certain association): up to now Peter has caught fish; now, however, he is to be a fisher of men – in the name of Jesus.

It is in fact interesting that we come across these particular words as a saying to Peter in another, very similar context. The story of the miraculous draught in Luke 5 displays many parallels to John 21. Luke 5.10 runs: 'And Jesus said to Simon, "Do not be afraid; henceforth you will be catching men." ' But in the context of Luke's Gospel Peter does not immediately become a fisher of men (as would really be expected from the 'henceforth'). He did, however, become so after Easter. It therefore seems to be a justifiable assumption that in Luke 5.1-11 we have to do with an Easter story which has been antedated – thrust back into the lifetime of Jesus. But then it is legitimate to ask whether the saying to Peter about being girded by another is a late form of the saying about his being a fisher of men. This kind of thing is never open to proof; but the similarity of the *motifs* makes it a reasonable supposition. The missionary charge to the eleven (or the disciples as the case may be) is also, after all, to be found in varying form; and we have seen that the important thing is not verbal similarity but similarity of meaning and intention in the face of different wording. Our story, then, contains two functional elements: the guidance (or gathering and guidance) of the church; and mission.

These two elements are found parallel to one another elsewhere as well. At the appearance of Jesus to the disciples in John 20.19-23 the missionary charge is followed by something like a commission of authority (the power to forgive sins), though here it is given to all the disciples.

When one has noticed this clue, a further parallel soon comes to mind. According to Matt. 16.19, Peter is given power over the keys; in Matt. 18.18, however, this same power is given to the church, in almost the same words. Are these too Easter *motifs*, transferred back into the lifetime of Jesus? For of course one is bound to ask, who actually received the power over the keys, Peter or the church? But perhaps it is wrong to formulate this question as an alternative. We could perhaps be hearing the echo of two successive events. Peter was commissioned first of all, the commission later being transferred to the church.

But is this fact connected with the priority of the appearance to Peter? Is there here too a reflection of successive events: Jesus appeared first to Peter and then to the twelve? These are all questions to which one is inclined to answer 'yes'. The point would then be the transmission of functions.

But however that may be, in the full story of the appearance to Peter (which lies behind John 21) the functional aspect was explicit from the very first. Is the same true of the Peter traditions which are available to us in formula-like phraseology?

Luke 24.34 is of particular interest in this connection. There we are told that the disciples (in Jerusalem according to Luke) have come to believe although up to now Jesus has only appeared to Peter. They cry to the Emmaus disciples on their return, 'The Lord has risen indeed, and has appeared to Simon!' They say this, obviously believing in their risen Lord, before they have personally experienced any appearance. That only comes later.

Now we must not, of course, forget what we said earlier: the order of the appearances in the Gospels is to be put down to the evangelists. All we can say about Luke 24.34 is that *according to Luke's Gospel itself* the disciples believed before Jesus had appeared to them. Whether this was actually the case we are not yet in a position to say.

But this observation about Luke brings us to another point. We may assume that the fact that Peter was the first to believe in the risen Lord was a piece of knowledge long cherished in the early Church. As we have seen, he is the first even in John, although there the priority is associated with the first entry into the empty tomb, not with a first appearance. Even though this incident is almost certainly unhistorical, it brings out the priority of Peter's *faith*. There is therefore no reason to doubt that Peter really was the first to believe in Jesus after Good Friday.

This, however, divides Peter from the others – at least in time. They arrived at belief later. In the oldest traditions available to us we are told that Peter believed because he saw Jesus. It may now be asked: did Peter first keep this appearance to himself, waiting to pass on the news until others (the eleven – or only the ten?) had said 'Jesus has appeared to us', his purpose being to emphasize that Jesus had appeared to him first of all? Or had he told the others about the appearance (and of course his belief) already?

The first alternative seems to me quite inconceivable. But in that case Peter was not only the first to believe; he also talked to the others about his experience. Did those who heard Peter's announcement also believe because of it? Luke says that they did; although admittedly he is alone in this.

With this we have arrived at a question which is of the greatest importance for our whole theme: did Jesus have to appear to the others before they were able to believe?

Of course I am well aware that this question cannot be precisely answered. Who is to say what is necessary? Yet the question has a heuristic value, because it helps us to discover what the 'vision' accomplishes (in any given case) and what it does not, or no longer needs to, accomplish. For anyone who maintains that Jesus had to appear to the other disciples before they were able to believe must be consistent. He must then be prepared to agree that nobody can find faith, even at the present day, unless he has experienced an appearance of Jesus. But this is a proposition which hardly anyone would maintain.

Even with the second appearance we already have the problem, so to speak, in reverse. Why is this appearance described at all, since the eleven (or ten) already believed? It is not the appearance itself which is a problem here; the problem is why an appearance was necessary for believers at all. It is not their 'having seen' which is a problem; the difficulty is why their having seen is especially mentioned, since this was not constitutive for their faith.

The same question then arises in the case of all the other appearances – to over five hundred brethren, to James and to all the apostles. Why are they mentioned at all? Only Paul is to some extent an exception.

One can evade the question by way of two different answers. One can say that the ten were particularly sceptical (more sceptical than we are, since we, after all, believe without any appearance). They were all like Thomas and so an appearance was necessary. But this answer will hardly be thought satisfactory. Alternatively one might say that the appearances really happened, so why should they not be reported? This may be admitted. But it is essential to add that an appearance was not necessary in order that the ten should believe; for they believed before. And this means that their faith too was dependent on the appearance to Peter.

We can therefore now answer the question put earlier. Since the appearance to Peter led others to faith, the functional aspect was bound up with this first appearance from the very beginning. Any other answer seems to me inconceivable. So although the functional aspect is not expressly named in the formula ('Jesus appeared to Peter'), the function is none the less implicit and is to be read into it. This is at least true of the first part of the formula.

Is it also true of the other sections? (For we left on one side the question of whether the functional aspect is implicit in the second part, 'Jesus appeared to the twelve'.) One could try to answer the question in the affirmative by pointing to the parallel structure of the different parts of the formula, for the echo at once suggests a similarity of interpretation.

This supposition can be supported if one looks more closely at the group of people who experienced the appearances. I have already drawn attention to certain peculiarities. The twelve are mentioned, but not the eleven. The relationship of the twelve to all the apostles is not clear; the two groups overlap, at least in part. And are we to imagine that the 'more than five hundred brethren' were a closed group to which neither the apostles, nor the twelve, nor Peter belonged? Were there therefore double appearances? How many did Peter experience? A profusion of ideas, suppositions and hypotheses have been put forward by scholars in answer to these questions but they have all continued to be disputed.

Instead of looking for new answers or trying to find a more solid foundation for the old ones, it would be better to consider why there is so much uncertainty at this point. This means basically: if, in spite of all attempts, there is no consensus of opinion about the answer, it is worth considering whether there is something wrong with the question itself – whether it is perhaps wrongly formulated or even inappropriate in itself. And this is, in my opinion, the case. The question is always put in directly historical terms: in what order did the appearances take place? Who was present and how often? The first question is never: why is this told at all? If one does ask this question, the answer is, I believe, easy enough to find.

Let me first split the question up into its component parts. Why are we told that there was an appearance to the twelve? Why are we told that there was an appearance to more than five hundred brethren? Why are we told the same thing of James? And why of the other apostles?

Apparently there was in the primitive church a group of the twelve. Their function is not exactly clear, but they were probably the bearers of the Jesus tradition. In addition there was a group of apostles. Their function was undoubtedly primarily a missionary one. We know that James was, after Peter, the leader of the church in Jerusalem. His function was therefore to direct. The group of more than five hundred brethren is somewhat nebulous. But would we be very far wrong if we supposed that we are here dealing with the whole church (at a particular time and perhaps also in a particular place)? The membership of these existing groups would frequently overlap. Some Christians would belong to two of them, some perhaps even to three. We can no longer be certain of the details.

We can now go on to ask: why are we told that all these different groups experienced an appearance of Jesus? What is the point of the narrative? I think it is this: their faith, the manifold functions which they exercised, are all in the ultimate resort based on the first appearance to Peter. They are all summed up in this appearance.

In saying this I am by no means asserting that there was only one appearance. (We have in any case still to consider the special case of the appearance to Paul.) We must only be methodologically clear about the following: *we* are always quick to ask, what happened? And of course I do not want to sweep aside this question. It can be put, like any other. But – methodologically – it has to be noted that before we can expect to receive an answer to this question we must first clarify *why* the story is told at all. We must be clear about what the authors of the texts wanted to say. Suppose we discover that the starting point for the wording of our formula is not the event but the groups which were (later) to be found in the church – an 'event' being deduced from these groups, through a process of *a posteriori* reasoning: in this case *direct* access to the event is barred to us.

Now it can of course be maintained that I am acting arbitrarily in taking as a starting point not the event itself but the groups whom we are told experienced a particular event. But this arbitrariness is no greater than if one proceeds in the opposite direction. Both approaches are based on hypotheses. The question is only who can justify the hypothesis of his choice.

In my opinion it can be demonstrated that the different parts of our formula have to be understood from the angle of the church. This is shown most clearly by the mention of the twelve. We have already seen that, in the appearance stories at the end of the Gospels, talk is always of the eleven (where a number is mentioned at all). From the point of view of the evangelists, it was indeed only possible to speak of the eleven disciples, after Judas had left them. But why does the formula speak of the twelve, in apparent disregard of the – admittedly later – story of the passion?

Let me make a small digression here. It is a much discussed question (and one on which there is still no consensus of opinion)

whether the group of the twelve goes back to the lifetime of Jesus
or whether it only came into being in the early church. If the
latter is the case, then the group was certainly not formed immediately after Good Friday. This would then be proof enough that
the formula takes its starting point from the church, not from the
appearance. But that is merely a hypothesis. Instead of taking the
easy way out which it offers, let us be really cautious and assume
the opposite position for the moment. According to this, Jesus called
the twelve during his earthly lifetime. Before the passion Judas fell
out. Later the group was supplemented through a new election. But
it is Acts alone which reports this, telling us that the election took
place only after Jesus' ascension (1.15-26). But by that time (at least
according to Luke) the appearances had come to an end. For this
reason there can have been no appearances to the twelve in Luke.

It might now be objected that Acts was misinformed here and
that the new election had taken place earlier. But even if one
concedes this, the election of Matthias cannot possibly have taken
place before the appearance to Peter, because at that time there was
as yet no need for a new election. If it took place immediately
afterwards, then the group of the twelve owed its *existence* at least
to the appearance to Peter. It did not owe its existence to the appearance to the twelve.

Again, it can of course be maintained that once the group was
in existence, it experienced an appearance. Obviously I cannot deny
this possibility. But it does not alter the fact that this group of
(what were now) believers did not owe its existence to this appearance. Only the appearance to Peter was constitutive.

It cannot, therefore, be denied that the faith of the twelve (*sic*) did
not take its origin from the appearance of Jesus *to them personally*,
but originated solely in the appearance to Peter. And this shows us
that the formula, in speaking of the twelve, was conceived from
the starting point of believers; and that means from the *existing*
church. It cannot be intending to prove that seeing Jesus was constitutive for the group of the twelve.

If we remain true to this angle of approach (starting from
the group of people involved) then various difficulties about the

formula disappear – difficulties which have often been felt but have never been satisfactorily solved. We no longer have to assume that there were a number of different appearances to Peter (first alone, then in the group of the twelve, then with all the apostles, and meanwhile perhaps with the 'more than five hundred brethren' as well). This has continually led to the question of what significance the later appearances had for Peter, since they could no longer be constitutive of his faith.

Nor is it necessary any longer to find ingenious solutions for the appearance to 'all the apostles'. Were these assembled by chance, all of them already *being* apostles? Or were there individual appearances which have been added together, so to speak, and so described as the appearance to all the apostles? Both these solutions can be tried out, but if we are prepared to think logically we soon come up against new difficulties.

The matter becomes much simpler if we turn the question round, as I have tried to do, and start from the church. According to this solution the twelve were the bearers of the Jesus tradition, but they did not all carry on missionary activity. A group then crystallized out which carried out the missionary work: Peter, some of the twelve, and others. These were the apostles. But one must now answer the question of why they carried out this missionary activity. The answer we are given is: they had seen Jesus.

If then, instead of wilfully asking what happened (because one is approaching the texts with one's own interests in mind), one first switches over to the question of why the story is told at all (because one wants to arrive at a methodologically tenable result), the following answer emerges: there were these groups in the early church (undoubtedly in succession); and there were particular functions (some of them individual functions). The list given in the formula, however, does not only serve the purpose of recounting Jesus' repeated appearance to ever-varying people and groups; on the contrary, the different people and groups are to be drawn together in that the same thing is said of all of them: they saw Jesus.

And this is just the way in which Paul also uses the formula. True, he adds himself to the list of those who have seen. But this is clearly not in order to say: 'Finally there was a further appearance to me myself.' The reason, once again, is exactly the opposite. Paul wants to include himself in the group. He wants to say that he too belongs to this very same circle, even though he had once been the persecutor of the church. ('Whether then it was I or they, so we preach and so you believed'; I Cor. 15.11.)

To avoid any misunderstanding, let me repeat once more that I am by no means asserting that there was only one appearance, the appearance to Peter. That could not be proved. But we must at all events establish that the formula is not aiming to *report the number* of the appearances. Its intention is to trace back the later functions and the later faith of the church, as well as the later leadership of James, to the one single root: the appearance of Jesus. This appearance, however, happened first to Peter. Summing up what we have said, therefore, we can briefly formulate the matter as follows: as far as Peter was concerned, seeing Jesus resulted in mission. The formula, however, is intended to convey that the mission derives from the seeing and has its basis there (mission being in this case an expression comprising various functions).

The functional aspect is therefore undoubtedly present in the formula. Its starting point is not the 'vision' of Jesus but the persons and groups whose functions are grounded on that vision.

Even if there were other appearances later (which can neither be ruled out nor, on the other hand, definitely asserted) the first did not simply and exclusively have the significance of temporal priority; it had priority of content also. It evoked faith in Simon so that he became Peter, a rock. His faith also led the others to faith; and for that reason the early church evolved the formula: 'The Lord has risen indeed, and has appeared to Simon' (Luke 24.34). But the knowledge that Simon Peter was the first was lodged in the later traditions in highly varying ways – even to the point of telling that, although he was second at the tomb in the disciples' race, he was the first to enter.

With this we may be said to have reached a more or less firm historical result. Let me try to formulate it as precisely as possible. After Good Friday Simon was the first who arrived at faith in

Jesus. But we must not phrase this historical conclusion as: Simon was the first to see Jesus. The relationship between believing and seeing must be expressed as follows: Simon was the first to believe; the reason for his having believed is expressed by saying that Simon saw Jesus.

We must be clear about the fact this historical enquiry has not brought us *direct* access to the vision of Simon. The only thing that is historically accessible is Simon's faith, not in the sense of its character as inner event (for this is obviously beyond our reach as well) but in its formative function for the church. In saying that one must make a clear distinction between these two things. I am not denying that Simon saw Jesus. But according to what we have said up to now it is impossible to assert the actual reality of the vision *itself*. The pattern is rather as follows: to the question of what can be established by historical investigation, we can only answer – the faith of Simon as constitutive of the church, and the *assertion* of the early church that this faith was grounded on the seeing of Jesus.

With this we have come to a turning point in our lectures. Here three different strands separate out, all of which we shall have to follow up.

1. We have now worked through the, at first sight, confusing Easter traditions and by stripping them down to their essentials have arrived at a single point: Peter's having believed. This raises the question – can the later tradition really be adequately explained on the basis of this single point? Is it possible to show how the later statements can be traced back to this point? And do these later statements really repeat what was implicit there? To put the question in concrete terms: can Peter's faith explain the story of the empty tomb? Or is the empty tomb enough to shake our conclusions? These questions show that the attempt to illuminate the later traditions from this one point is also a test of the accuracy of our results.

2. We must remember that the subject of our lectures is: the resurrection of Jesus of Nazareth. But we have reached our present turning point without having come in sight of the resurrection

at all. It is certainly mentioned in the early confession of faith in Luke 24.34; but we ourselves have only discussed the seeing of Jesus. The question thus arises: in what relationship does the alleged 'vision' of Peter stand to the credal assertion that 'Jesus is risen'?

3. In order to be able to answer this question we must explain how we are to think of this vision and what its nature was. Let me remind you that while we were considering the Gospels we asked several times whether it is possible to discover from the way in which the appearances are related what must have happened for them to be possible. But this proved impossible because of the wide differences in the appearance narratives. Can we draw this *a posteriori* conclusion now?

The third problem would seem to offer the best starting point. Admittedly there is a difficulty here. We cannot ask Peter himself, for there is no testimony which derives directly from him. We only have the testimonies of others who claim that Peter saw Jesus. But we do know a man belonging to the early church who made the direct assertion that he himself had seen Jesus: Paul. So it would seem a reasonable plan to begin with him.

IV The 'Vision' of Paul

We shall start from the point where the vision of Peter and the vision of Paul are named in juxtaposition – that is to say, where there seems to be a connection between the two: I Cor. 15.5 and 8. In both cases the Greek word ὤφθη is used.

Attempts have often been made to find an explanation of the vision by drawing on the grammatical form used (aorist passive). But [unfortunately there are a number of possible ways of translating the Greek.] The simplest would be to read (he was seen). But if one assumes the deponent meaning (which is a possibility) it could be translated 'he appeared' or 'he allowed himself to be seen' or 'he showed himself'. But the passive can also be interpreted as a way of avoiding the utterance of the divine name; this was a common Jewish practice. In this case one could translate the phrase as 'God revealed'. We can see, therefore, (that this single word is open to a great number of interpretations.] (Let me digress for a moment in order to draw your attention to another point. I have just said that 'we can see . . .' Have we really 'seen' anything? But I can still use the word here, in a completely comprehensible way. And this meaning can be associated with the word 'see' in Greek as well.)

Which of the possible meanings are we now to take? Scholars are divided on this point. Since, as we have said, we cannot ask Peter directly, let us see whether Paul's statement can take us any further, for he says that he too experienced an ὤφθη (I Cor. 15.8). Of course this ὤφθη is later and not identical with Peter's. But it is significant that Paul can also describe his experience by means of the word ὤφθη, thus putting it in the same category as Peter's. So although it cannot tell us the nature of Peter's ὤφθη, it can perhaps tell us how Paul interpreted it. Whether he interpreted it correctly is of course another question. But we will at least learn how a man of the same period, familiar with its language and concepts, thought it possible and permissible to interpret this vision.

Now, of course, we should be no further forward if we only found this one term in Paul. But since Paul uses different terminology in another passage, even though he is obviously still thinking of the same event, a comparison could be helpful.

This method has often been used before. But unfortunately it has nearly always been applied too directly. In the interests of quick results, not enough care has always been taken to choose the approach capable of yielding findings which would stand up to examination. I do not want to make my argument too protracted, but on the other hand we must proceed cautiously if we are not to run into a *cul de sac*, especially since we cannot divide our problem (what did Paul mean when he spoke of seeing Jesus?) from the problem of the relationship in Paul between his 'vision' and his assertion of the resurrection of Jesus.

It is sometimes said that his experience on the Damascus road was Paul's Easter. This seems an obvious formulation, because in the list of witnesses given in I Cor. 15 every vision is related to the resurrection. But we have seen that this interpretation is not without its problems, because from the second section of the formula onwards the seeing has no constitutive significance for faith in the risen Lord; that was true only of Peter's experience. But what is the position with regard to Paul? If one speaks here of an Easter experience, one must ask how 'Easter' could be experienced years later? And this means that we must first decide the place which Paul holds in the framework of the whole tradition of the Easter proclamation; we must not immediately ask directly about his experience on the Damascus road.

Paul was a persecutor of the church. This presupposes that he was, broadly speaking, informed about the church's purpose and character. He must therefore have known what its message was and how its members conducted themselves because of that message. What did Paul know?

We sometimes hear it said that the apostle was offended by the Christian proclamation of the crucified Jesus as Messiah. But there is no passage where Paul gives this as the reason for his earlier persecution. The texts rather suggest that the real point of controversy was the church's critical attitude to the law. By calling in question the law's validity, Christianity was a danger for Judaism, as Paul, the Pharisee, realized. The messianic claim at most only played a part in the persecution in so far as it was the reason for Christian criticism of the law. It was not in itself the motive for Paul's attitude.

In this connection it must now be asked whether Paul also knew the Christian assertion of Jesus' resurrection. This too would have been no reason for persecution except again in so far as it was a ground for Christian criticism of the law.

It is impossible to be completely certain whether Paul had already heard of Jesus' resurrection at the time when he was persecuting the church. This may seem to us astonishing, for we think of it as being a matter of course. But we must abide by the fact that we have no knowledge on the point, at least not directly.

Is it possible to arrive at any indirect conclusion? This is difficult because the extant Pauline epistles belong to a much later period. The earliest (I Thessalonians) was written more than a decade after his experience on the Damascus road. Now it is noticeable here (and in the later letters too) that Paul frequently mentions the resurrection of Jesus in contexts which clearly bear a formalized character and therefore probably do not originally derive from Paul himself. When he took over these formalized phrases, however, is an unsolved question. He could have come across them after he had already become a Christian. So it is in fact conceivable that Paul was a Christian before he heard about the resurrection of Jesus. I myself think that this is improbable, but anything we cannot be sure of must be left open.

However, this reflection may be of help to us. For we must ask how Paul relates his experience on the Damascus road to statements about the resurrection of Jesus. The two are only associated with one another in I Cor. 15, curiously enough; and there the reason is that Paul links his ὤφθη on to the formulation which already existed. And this formulation spoke of the resurrection.

We have therefore the curious fact that although nearly all his letters mention Jesus' resurrection in some connection or other (even if not nearly as frequently as is generally thought), Paul him-

self does not associate the resurrection with his experience on the
Damascus road. This seems to me important in so far as Paul therefore fails to indicate whether it was that experience which convinced
him of Jesus' resurrection. The two traditions (the Damascus road
and the resurrection) run parallel to one another in a curiously unrelated way. I Cor. 15 is the only exception. And that too is only
apparently an exception, for Paul is linking up his vision with the
vision of others; and these earlier visions were in fact connected with
the resurrection.

Let us now look first at the passages where Paul speaks of his
Damascus road experience, taking the epistles in chronological order.

He first mentions his experience in Gal. 1.15-17. In the Authorized
Version the passage runs like this: 'But when it pleased God, who
separated me from my mother's womb, and called me by his grace,
to reveal ($\dot{\alpha}\pi o\kappa\alpha\lambda\dot{\upsilon}\psi\alpha\iota$) his Son in me, that I might preach him
among the heathen; immediately I conferred not with flesh and
blood: neither went I up to Jerusalem to them which were apostles
before me; but I went into Arabia . . .'

This is an extremely curious passage. At first sight it agrees with
I Cor. 15.10 in its stressing of the functional aspect. Paul knows that
the Damascus road experience has sent him to preach among the
Gentiles. But the odd thing is that Paul does not here speak of
seeing Jesus; he speaks of God's having revealed his Son in him.
Much thought has been expended on this passage. Frequent attempts
have been made, naturally, to interpret the 'revealing' in terms of
an appearance, the aim being to avoid the difficulties which arise
when one interprets the statement in the sense of a subjective vision.
Stress has been laid on the fact that more is being claimed than a
mental experience on Paul's part, more than a sudden awareness or
overwhelming conviction of the truth of the Christian message.
Other passages have been drawn upon, where Paul speaks of seeing,
setting this on a level with seeing on the part of other people. Since
this latter seeing is not merely with the mind's eye, Paul cannot
mean this in Gal. 1.16 either. But one cannot argue like this. It is
methodologically inadmissible to conclude anything about the 'reveal
in me' from the 'seeing' of other people, especially when the nature

of this seeing is by no means established. (The 'in me' must not, incidentally, be pressed. It is grammatically possible – though not necessary – to read the form as a dative and to translate it as 'God revealed his Son *to* me'; cf. the Revised Standard Version.)

Let us not give way to speculation but abide by what can be said with certainty. When Paul speaks of his Damascus experience he does not *have* to use the word 'see'. He can describe it by means of another term whose general meaning is the uncovering of something which is otherwise – or has been up to now – hidden. The term leaves the mode of this uncovering completely open.

If we only possessed this account of his Damascus experience, we would never suppose that Paul became a Christian because he saw Jesus. It might perhaps be said that he was familiar with the Christian proclamation and, having first rejected it, was later overwhelmed by its message. The truth was uncovered, or revealed to him. Paul was expressing this in the words: God revealed his Son in (or to) me.

The curious thing is this. In the context of Gal. 1 and 2 Paul's purpose is to establish the direct nature of his apostleship (and hence his independence of Jerusalem). If we now ask how Paul could, in our opinion, have best succeeded in this, we should probably answer that he ought to have argued as follows: 'You say that my apostleship is dependent on Jerusalem? You are wrong; for just as *they* saw Jesus, so *I* saw him too.' In this way he would have established the direct and independent nature of his apostleship.

But this is not quite the way in which Paul argues. He mentions his experience, using the word 'reveal', and displays his independence of Jerusalem by stressing: 'I was a persecutor of the church; and even after the revelation I received, I did not go straight to Jerusalem, to those who were already apostles; I spoke to no one, but at once went to preach the gospel in Arabia.' (We can deduce the fact that Paul was a missionary in Arabia from the fact that we know him to have been persecuted by the ethnarchs of King Aretas, as recorded in II Cor. 11.32f.) Paul therefore proves his independence by showing that he began his missionary work without reference to Jerusalem.

In the next passage we shall look at (I Cor. 9.1f.). Paul calls his experience 'seeing' for the first time:

Am I not free? Am I not an apostle? Have I not seen (ἑώρακα) Jesus our Lord? Are you not my workmanship in the Lord? If to others I am not an apostle, at least I am to you; for you are the seal of my apostleship in the Lord.

Again it is immediately evident that Paul associates this experience, which he calls seeing Jesus, with his apostolic function. One must also note that this passage too is apologetic in character, although the defence has a somewhat different tendency from that of the epistle to the Galatians. There the point was the direct authority of Paul's apostleship; here it is the *fact* of his apostleship. The apostleship of the others is apparently undisputed (or Paul believes that this is so). People are sitting in judgment on Paul, he says in v. 3. They want to deny him liberty; and in v. 5 he points to the freedom claimed by 'the other apostles and the brothers of the Lord and Cephas'. The aim of Paul's defence is to express his membership of this circle. But he grounds this claim on the fact that he too has seen Jesus.

But now a question arises. How can he convince the Corinthians that he has really seen Jesus? In the case of the Galatians things were different. There Paul could prove his independence of Jerusalem by naming the places where he had been – among which Jerusalem was not included. If necessary that could be verified; and then Paul's statement would have to be accepted. But he cannot use this argument to the Corinthians. He cannot point to any verifiable facts. For although Paul bases his claim to apostleship on the statement that he has seen Jesus, his opponents could reply that this was merely an assertion which he was incapable of proving. Nor does Paul make any attempt at proof, knowing that such an attempt would inevitably be unsuccessful. The evidence that he offers is of a different kind, that 'of the Spirit and [of] power'. 'If to others I am not an apostle, at least I am to you; for you are the seal of my apostleship in the Lord.'

In other words Paul reminds the Corinthians that they have become the church of Jesus through his labours. Something happened to them. They found faith. The proof of the Spirit and of power was shown in Corinth through Paul's preaching. And since the Corinthians have experienced this they must admit that Paul is truly their apostle and that his apostleship cannot be called in question. If others want to dispute this apostleship, they can. They even have a certain right to do so, for these others have not become Christians through him. Therefore they *cannot* say that he is an apostle. Only the man who has believed because of Paul's ministry can experience and maintain the authenticity of his apostleship.

The position which Paul gives to his experience on the Damascus road can only be deduced from the context as a whole, not merely from his mention of the vision. For Paul the experience meant a great deal; but by itself it was still not a sufficient argument. It would not have been one even if he had described his experience in every detail. Even this would not have been *completely* convincing. So he remains within the framework of what he finds really important, merely giving this brief indication: I have seen Jesus our Lord.

This leads us to an intermediary question: are we today (at all events in our theological discussion) perhaps concentrating on a point which – at least in Paul's argument – does not play at all the part which we generally suppose? In modern terminology we might put it as follows: *historically* Paul bases his apostleship on his experience on the Damascus road; but *theologically* he bases it on the existence of the church. The historical foundation has no meaning taken in isolation – no meaning, that is, capable of settling anything by itself. Finally, let me point out that there is once again no mention of the resurrection of Jesus in this context.

That the resurrection is finally mentioned in the last of the passages before us (I Cor. 15.8) is on the one hand due to the problem which is being treated in this chapter; and on the other hand, as we showed earlier, it is connected with the formulation which Paul quotes. The ὤφθη in v. 8 does not indicate a particular characterization of his experience on Paul's part, however; he is simply making use of the term which already exists.

Let us ask once more what the nature of Paul's vision was. We cannot draw on the ὤφθη of I Cor. 15.8 for the reasons we have given. There remain two phrases: 'God revealed his Son (in or to) me' and 'I have seen Jesus our Lord'. But these do not take us very far. The only thing about which we can be certain is that Paul does not feel *bound* to characterize his experience as seeing.

We can now direct our questions into two different channels: on the one hand, did Paul see Jesus and then (for whatever reason) call this experience a revelation (in Gal. 1.16)? or did he originally leave the nature of his experience open and only later speak of 'seeing', perhaps so that he could incorporate his *revelation* in the *seeing* claimed by the others? It is of course impossible to prove anything here. But there are a few indications.

It can be shown, for example, that Paul did not use the word 'reveal' in Gal. 1.16 more or less by chance but that he was probably using a characteristic turn of phrase. He has already used the same term immediately before. In Gal. 1.11f. he says that the gospel which he has preached is not an earthly one; he has not received it, or learnt it, from men but 'through a revelation of Jesus Christ'. He obviously cannot mean that the content of his preaching was communicated to him in a supernatural message outside Damascus. He already knew the message (at least in part) while he was still the persecutor of the church. But that this message was the gospel, and not (or not merely, as we should say) human words – this was not brought home to him by human agency but by 'a revelation of Jesus Christ'. One may therefore at least suspect that Paul earlier described his experience in provisional and general terms as a revelation. The further defining of this revelation as seeing only came about through assimilation to what was (probably) common linguistic usage. The possibility of an assimilation of this kind cannot be excluded, for we know that Paul certainly practised it in I Cor. 15.8 (this time with the help of the term ὤφθη).

In this case Paul's shift of terminology would show something very similar to what we saw happening earlier (in I Cor. 15.5-7) with the links in the chain of appearance witnesses. Existing functions whatever their origin) are legitimized through a 'having seen' which had its origin in the first 'having seen' of Peter. At all events, in the series of Pauline formulations there is an increasing conformity to the formulations of the tradition. One can take this as mere chance and say: Paul *did* see Jesus on the Damascus road. That would be one hypothesis. But one can also say: As time went on Paul was constrained, for apologetic reasons, to approximate his formulations to those of tradition. This would be another hypothesis, which is admittedly not dependent on chance but has at least a certain amount of evidence in its favour. However, both remain hypotheses. For that reason we cannot discover what really happened on the Damascus road. Persecutor became preacher; but *how* exactly can no longer be arrived at. It is better to admit this fact at once and not to try to conceal our lack of knowledge through mere assertion.

Paul evidently did not think it necessary to inform his readers about the precise nature of his experience. One thing is apparent, however. Whatever it was that Paul experienced, he says here: *God* did something to me. That is why his gospel is not human in kind but of divine origin. Paul wants to say (to put it in quite simple terms) that he has received some external impact and that this impact came from God.

Paul can confess that it was God who acted on him, but he is naturally unable to prove it. So he turns to the only place where proof can be found – in the church. Wherever the church believes, it knows that Paul's gospel comes from God and is not his own. The church could not be more certain of this fact even if Paul were to describe his experience in its every detail. It would then be informed about the way in which faith was born in Paul, but this information could not form the ground of the church's own faith. So it is in line with the nature of the matter when Paul only touches on his Damascus road experience, though maintaining the divine origin of his gospel. But the members of the church *can* only experience this when they themselves believe – on the basis of that gospel.

But we must now look again at the question of the relationship of this experience to Paul's preaching of the resurrection of Jesus.

We have already established one negative result – that Paul nowhere gives us to understand that what happened to him on the Damascus road convinced him that Jesus was risen. It is therefore wrong to call this experience 'Paul's Easter' – unless one understands by Easter the experience of finding faith in Jesus. In this sense one could of course speak of an Easter in the case of many Christians. But that does not make them witnesses of Jesus' resurrection; nor is any vision necessary. Faith can be born in very varied ways. But it is always a 'revelation' in the sense that what has hitherto been held to be a human word reveals itself as the word of God, a word to which one now surrenders. One becomes aware of it, one 'sees' what one had never seen before – or however one likes to express the miracle (and it *is* a miracle!). But an Easter in this sense does not make any Christian a witness of the original resurrection of Jesus. And it did not make Paul one either. Can this experience, then, still be called Easter? Perhaps it is in fact the real Easter.

But let us first return to Paul. When people want to point out the importance of the resurrection for Paul, they frequently quote the sentence: 'If Christ has not been raised, then our *kerygma* (our preaching) is in vain and your faith is in vain' (I Cor. 15.14). If one takes this sentence apart from its context, one might really say that according to Paul absolutely everything hangs on the resurrection of Jesus as an actual event. If the resurrection had no factual reality, then preaching is empty and faith is no longer possible. Even if we agreed that Paul meant this, we must hold fast to two things. First, we still do not learn directly what Paul meant by the resurrection of Jesus. Secondly, we still should not know how Paul had learnt about Jesus' resurrection, since his experience on the Damascus road (which took place years later) did not make him a witness of that resurrection. He can only have heard about it in some other way. So even if Paul meant to say that the resurrection, as a factual event, was the essential prerequisite for the existence of preaching and faith, the resurrection would still remain an assertion on Paul's part. We should then have to ask him how he knew about it. It is true that he says a little later, 'But in fact Christ *has* been raised from the dead . . .' (I Cor. 15.20); but this too still remains a mere assertion.

In any case, however, it is wrong to separate the sentence in I Cor. 15.14 from its context. Let us look at this context for a moment. Paul goes on to say that the preachers of the gospel would *then* be false witnesses; they would *then* have misrepresented God in saying that he had raised Christ, whom he had not raised (could not have raised) if it is true that the dead are not raised. If, therefore, Christ has not been raised, then the faith of the Corinthians is futile and they are still in their sins (cf. I Cor. 15.15-17).

If one looks at the context as a whole, one sees that Paul is talking the whole time about a hypothetical case. He is pointing out the consequences which would arise if the premise were correct. That is to say, Paul is addressing the Corinthians in this way on the assumption that the hypothetical case does not apply. To reformulate his words in positive terms, he says: you believe; you have experienced the forgiveness of sins. So our preaching *has* a genuine content and we *cannot* be false witnesses.

The situation is therefore as follows. The people in Corinth who deny the resurrection of the dead must, to be consistent, also deny the resurrection of Jesus (I Cor. 15.13). But the resurrection of Jesus has been preached to them and this preaching has been effective (I Cor. 15.11). The Corinthians would therefore have to deny something of whose truth they are fully aware: that they themselves are Christians; that they themselves believe; that they themselves have experienced the forgiveness of sins.

If one takes the context into account one realizes that Paul is not here offering anything in the nature of factual evidence for the resurrection (which he was not in a position to do in any case). He is marshalling a proof within the framework of a particular theological logic. It runs like this: since you know that you have found faith, you are bound to admit that your faith has a presupposition. Paul does not therefore assume the *a priori* certainty of a particular presupposition, then going on to argue from this presupposition: since the presupposition is certain, the results must also be true. On the contrary, Paul argues from the results themselves. Since these results are undisputed (as the Corinthians know) the presupposition must be correct as well.

Is this argument valid? Indeed, is this *method* of argument admissible at all? In concrete terms – can one deduce the factual nature of the resurrection from the existence of faith – faith which one shares oneself? I have already shown that faith cannot serve as an instrument of knowledge about past events, for that is not its nature.

Keeping this question in mind, let us turn back to I Cor. 9.1f. for a moment. The point at issue there was Paul's apostleship. We saw that the reason that he gave in substantiation was that the Corinthians were the seal of his apostleship. In as much as they believe, they experience the truth that Paul's gospel is from God. Paul might also have phrased his point as follows: 'If I were not an apostle sent by God, my preaching would be vain; and in this case your faith would also be vain. But you know that your faith is not vain and this tells you that I am your apostle, sent by God.'

Common to both 'proofs' is the presupposition that faith has a source and that the source is God. That the source is God can only be discovered through faith. To put it in theological terms – faith has an *extra nos*, i.e., something outside ourselves. We now see that Paul can express this *extra nos* in various ways: in I Cor. 9.1f. by means of his apostleship; in I Cor. 15.14-17 by means of the proclamation of Jesus' resurrection. The structure of the argument remains the same. The starting point is always the thing that is certain: the faith of the church.

Let us now place the two logical progressions side by side. The argument in I Cor. 9 runs: the faith of the church – Paul's apostleship – the receiving of the apostolic function through the seeing of Jesus. The argument in I Cor. 15 runs: the faith of the church – the *preaching* of Jesus' resurrection – the resurrection.

We must now ask once more what the Corinthians could be sure of through faith. The answer is – in both cases, only the second link in the chain of argument. Through faith they experience the truth that Paul is an apostle sent from God. The way in which he came to be an apostle is already outside the truth of their faith; for though Paul can tell them this, it is purely a matter of information. The fact that he could formulate it in widely differing terms suggests that he did not consider the information to be of essential importance.

Now let us look at the second logical progression. What can the Corinthians be sure of here through faith? Merely that the *preaching* of the resurrection has led them to faith in Christ and that they have thereby experienced the truth of the forgiveness of sins. The historical facts behind the preaching of the resurrection could be told them (though they are not, in fact, told); but this is not part of the truth of their faith. It could at most be a matter of information.

Let me now come back to the question we passed over: can one deduce the resurrection of Jesus as a *factual event* from the existence of faith? The answer is an unequivocal no. On this point one can only be informed. But faith can give certainty about the truth of the *preaching* of the resurrection.

Does this differentiation between the *preaching* of the resurrection and the resurrection as an historical event lead us into the old dilemma? For what can the preaching of the resurrection be about if it is not about the resurrection itself? But let us remind ourselves of what we said earlier: the *preaching* of the resurrection can have as its content: 'Jesus lives and therefore he is of immediate concern to me.' And it is precisely this which Paul had evidently proclaimed to the Corinthians. If we make *this* our starting point, we can then go on to say: 'If Jesus were not alive, then this preaching would be vain.' But the content of the preaching of the resurrection does not have to include the *way* in which the crucified Jesus rose. Jesus can be experienced as 'he that liveth' in faith kindled through preaching. But faith cannot tell how he became alive.

Paul can hence tell his readers about his experience on the Damascus road (even though in varying terms). For he experienced it himself. He was a direct witness. But he was not a witness of the resurrection.

There is no doubt at all that Paul was convinced that the resurrection of Jesus had taken place. But neither in I Cor. 15 nor anywhere else does he offer factual evidence. Consequently one cannot appeal to Paul in any attempt to hold fast to the historical nature of Jesus' resurrection. Nor did the apostle use his experience on the Damascus road as factual evidence for the resurrection. The nature of his vision remains obscure. Hence the only direct witness known to us who claims to have seen Jesus falls away when we ask how we can work back from the seeing of Jesus to his resurrection. Thus we are once again thrown back on the ὤφθη which we are told was experienced by Peter.

V The Miracle of the Resurrection

The prospects of still arriving at Jesus' resurrection as a historical event, in spite of the failure of our earlier attempts, are not very promising. There are two reasons for this, one historical – our sources are extremely scanty – and one theological – the thing which we are looking for eludes our grasp.

Before I come to the source question, let me make one point in advance. The only direct witness to whom we could appeal was Paul. If even in his case we were unable to explain exactly the ὤφθη with which he finally (in I Cor. 15.8) paraphrased his Damascus experience, how are we to be any more successful with Peter's ὤφθη, to which we have only indirect testimony?

But before I go into this I should like to say something about the theological reason why it is difficult to arrive at the resurrection of Jesus. The reason is that we have to do with a miracle; and a miracle eludes one's grasp. This is not meant to be a magic formula on which we can fall back when we can go no further. But because that is precisely what people have often tried to do, let me first try to throw a little light on the problem involved. What we must not do is, first, to maintain that scholarship can achieve nothing, because we are dealing with a miracle – and then at once go on to describe the said miracle without giving any account of the way in which the description is to be arrived at. If we do this, the statement that we have to do with a miracle really does become an inadmissible magic formula. Nothing can be solved like this. We must go about the matter differently.

Let us again start off from what we have already said. At the very beginning of our lectures I drew your attention to the two emphases which are inherent in the statement 'Jesus is risen'. When the accent is on the present, the sentence can mean: 'Jesus is alive; consequently he is of immediate concern to me.' If the accent is laid on the past, the sentence can mean: 'God raised

Jesus from the dead on the third day.' Which of these two versions involves a miracle?

Probably the immediate answer will be that the miracle belongs to the past; for God's raising of Jesus from the dead is, after all, the miracle of miracles, or ranks as such. But this answer seems to me unduly hasty. In my opinion it must first of all be emphasized that the miracle is to be found where the stress lies on the present tense, or on contemporary faith. One might immediately counter: 'Is the past event, then, not a miracle at all?' I do not deny it, but it is impossible to recognize the miraculous character of an event belonging to the past. I can at most guess that it was a miracle – but *only* if I am acquainted with the corresponding miracle today.

I hope to be able to demonstrate this, and to demonstrate it by the breakdown of that very historical enquiry which we are again pursuing. Here we shall come across two facts which I shall first develop and then relate to one another.

1. On the one hand we have Peter's ὤφθη. We meet it in the form of an assertion which does not, however, derive from Peter himself (at least in the form in which it has come down to us) but which was framed by other people. Other people state that Jesus appeared to Simon. One must be precise at this point because otherwise it is easy for confusion to creep in, as is the case, for instance, if one simply says that Peter saw Jesus. I am not denying that he did; but we must not forget how we came to acquire this piece of knowledge. We acquired it through the assertion of other people.

This assertion could never be verified, not even during Peter's lifetime. But if someone had then heard that the Lord had appeared to Simon, he could at least have gone to Simon and asked whether it was true. We cannot even put the question. The information comes to us in the form of an assertion which has gone through at least two stages of transmission: Simon's own statement that he had seen Jesus and the statement of other people that Simon had seen him.

But even that must be defined more closely. I am not stressing

this out of any undue scepticism but simply in order to make clear
the methodological problem. When a sequence of events was being
described, the two stages of transmission could be mentioned
consecutively. But we must take account of the fact that *we* first
meet with the assertion of others; and *from this point can infer*
a possible assertion on the part of Simon. I say a *possible* assertion
deliberately. For we must reckon with the fact that Simon himself
may have expressed his experience in quite different terms. One
must not call this a merely theoretical possibility and reproach
people with dishonesty if they formulate the assertion differently
from the way in which Simon would perhaps have done. This
reproach would then have to be levied against Paul as well. For
we have seen that he first spoke of a revealing and later of a
seeing, meaning the same event – his coming to believe on the
Damascus road. So it is at least *conceivable* that Simon came to
believe and that others expressed this fact by saying that Jesus
had appeared to him.

These reflections show that even so seemingly secure a starting
point as the ὤφθη of Simon contains a not entirely uncompli-
cated problem – a problem which we must penetrate if we want
to arrive at clarity. There is no cutting of the Gordian knot –
it must be carefully untied. So I shall have to ask you to be patient.
We can only escape from the vast confusion which surrounds us
today if we proceed as cautiously as possible. Our present misunderstandings are nearly all due to the fact that we are unwilling
to take time for reflection.

2. On further enquiry we have acquired as a further datum the
assertion that Jesus is risen. This assertion, in as far as it means
a factual event of the past, can no longer be verified. Even if
one had lived in the first generation, there was no one who could
have been asked whether the event had really happened – whether
he was there and saw it. At least we know of no one in the primitive church who claimed to have witnessed the event. And we may
be fairly certain that we should know if there had been a witness.
Something is therefore being asserted for which no witnesses are
brought and for which probably none can be brought.

So much for these two pieces of data which we encountered in the course of our enquiry. It is clear that we are moving in a complex of tradition which we cannot entirely penetrate. But let us try to link up the two pieces of data.

Formally speaking, the two are already associated in Luke 24.34 and I Cor. 15.3-5; and here the problem mentioned above meets us once more. The sequence in the two statements is: risen – appeared. But this is, even at this point, clearly a reversal. The two assertions have been so linked together that the assertion for which no witnesses are named precedes the assertion for which Peter is presented as witness. This means, however, that *we* must again begin from the point nearest to us. We cannot therefore start from the resurrection or even from Simon's vision but, in precise terms, only from the assertion of other people that Simon had seen Jesus.

Here we again find the term ὤφθη as the only word in which the assertion is clothed. I have already said that there are a number of possible translations and that the question cannot be decided on philological grounds. But it is worth considering whether a philological explanation would tell us any more, factually speaking.

If we were dealing with a direct statement made by Peter to the effect that 'Jesus appeared to *me*' (or something along those lines), we could then, if the verb were clear, perhaps discover something more about the nature of the vision. But we are in fact dealing with a statement made by other people; and consequently, even if we could clear up the philological question, we should at most discover how these people expressed and interpreted Peter's vision. Again we must remember that Paul can use ὤφθη to formulate something which he expresses in another passage by the word 'reveal'.

If we are clear about this, it then becomes evident that it is fruitless to discuss the alternatives of a subjective and an objective vision, though this was common practice earlier and can still be found occasionally today.

According to the subjective vision theory, the seeing of Jesus was an event in the mind of Peter (and the disciples). Their seeing was, so to speak, a product of their faith. In this case belief in Jesus would have come first and this belief would have conjured up the vision – i.e., Peter already believed at the time when he saw Jesus. The vision would then have confirmed his already existing faith. No one will deny that something of this sort is conceivable or that it actually occurs.

But this theory would only have a point if we were dealing with Peter's personal statement. And in the case of Paul, where we really do have a personal statement, the explanation is quite untenable. Whether Paul actually saw Jesus on the Damascus road or not, it was Paul the persecutor of the church who had the experience, not Paul the believer. He believed because of his experience. There is no doubt that he intends to express the fact that the impulse to faith came from outside himself – and this, let me stress once more, whether he actually saw Jesus or not.

But even if we only have the indirect assertion of Peter that he had seen Jesus, it is impossible to deny that the people who formulated the assertion and passed it on also meant to say that it was an external impulse which led Peter to believe. Consequently a subjective vision hypothesis breaks down because it cannot be brought into accord with the texts. They are absolutely unequivocal. They at least intend to speak of an objective vision – if one presents them with the alternative.

But here we must beware of jumping to a dangerously hasty conclusion. We must not go on to say that this shows that the objective vision hypothesis must therefore be correct. This would be to place on one and the same plane something which is on two different levels in the tradition. The one plane is: other people say that Peter saw Jesus, that he received an impulse from outside himself. The other plane would be a statement made by Peter *himself*. So although other people *maintain* the objective vision, this does not of itself guarantee the fact that Peter's vision *was* an objective one.

Simply in order to make the problem clear (not because I am claiming that it was so) let me put the position in exaggerated hypothetical terms. It is conceivable that Peter merely imagined that he saw Jesus, although he was perhaps subjectively speaking honestly convinced that he did so. Later, people described this experience as an objective vision. All that is still available to us, therefore, is merely what people said later. And even though these people maintained that the vision was an objective one, this still does not bring us into contact with the objective vision itself.

Now it is no help at all if we bring God into the statement, interpreting the ὤφθη to mean that *God* revealed Jesus to human perception. This does not take us any further even if one were to understand this as being the statement of Peter himself. One could accept Peter's statement that he saw Jesus. But if he said that God had showed him the living Lord, that would be *his* explanation of the way in which the vision came about; but it would only be his *explanation*.

Attempts have been made to argue differently. It has been said that faith reckons with the action of God, deducing from this that we (in faith) can reckon with the fact that God was at work when Peter saw Jesus. Let us see what has happened here. My faith reckons with God's action. Every believer would agree with this. But my faith *today* cannot form an opinion as to whether *God* brought about Peter's vision *in the past*. This would be to allow my faith today to form a judgment about the objectivity of a vision in the past. This would, on the face of it, 'vindicate' the objectivity of Peter's vision; but the objective vision hypothesis has been unnoticeably harnessed to one's own subjective faith. What is therefore disguised as an objective vision hypothesis is thus really, if one looks closely enough, *also* subjective – only in this case the subjectivity is that of my own faith. In short, I believe; and my belief says that Peter really saw Jesus. But of course one simply cannot argue like that.

None the less, we are bound to ask what role faith does play in this whole context. I said earlier that I could say of a past event that it was a miracle only if I experienced a corresponding miracle today. If this is correct (and if miracle and faith belong together) then faith has to be introduced into the problem if we are to escape from the *cul de sac* into which we seem to have strayed.

I am honestly convinced that one can make progress here only if faith is brought into the matter. But one must note the exact limits of what faith can do in the context of this question. Sometimes approaches have been chosen which do not lead to the desired goal. It is worth going into these briefly, because we can learn from the mistakes that have been made. In general the focus of attention has been not Peter's vision but the resurrection of Jesus. But this is only an alteration in the objects one is seeking to discover. It makes no difference to the methodological problem.

It has sometimes been maintained that the resurrection of Jesus is an event beyond man's inherent cognitive capacity. In other words, Jesus' resurrection is an event which cannot be arrived at by the methods of historical research. But, it is stressed, this is not to relinquish the resurrection as a real event; nor is this necessary; for the resurrection is open to the perception of the spiritual man.

I do not deny that the spiritual man (which is to say the believer) can enjoy a particular kind of knowledge. But we must be clear about what he can know and what he can not. We can make this clear to ourselves by introducing a term (admittedly a very unfortunate one) which is often used in the context of this argument. People speak of the 'facts of redemption', numbering the resurrection among these. This phrase is supposed to designate a fact which vouches for my redemption, which brings me redemption, which happened *for* my redemption. The emphasis is on the word 'fact'; and it is then argued that once the factual character is lost it is no longer possible to speak of a fact of *redemption* at all. This seems at first obvious, but it obscures the real problem. Who is to decide that the fact of redemption is a fact at all (or, in our case, a real event)? Only a historian can do so.

Let me take an example. Jesus' words and deeds were an event that really happened – a fact, to use our present terminology. But that they were an event which took place for the redemption of mankind cannot of course be decided by a historian.

A few decades ago there was a school of thought which maintained that Jesus never lived, that he was a purely mythical figure.

This was a shock to many Christians at the time. I am of the opinion (and it is an opinion shared by every serious historian) that the theory is historically untenable. But this must be demonstrated by historical research. One cannot appeal to faith in the matter. We cannot, that is to say, argue that since Jesus means salvation for us, since we believe in him, he must have lived; and therefore the theory that he was a myth must be untenable. The faith which attempted this would exceed the bounds of its own potentialities. As long as I am concerning myself with facts, I must use the methods through whose help alone these facts can be established. What I believe to be a fact of *redemption* (for whatever reason) is not therefore necessarily a fact.

But one must see the other side of the shield as well. If we ask the historian whether Jesus rose from the dead and he answers 'No', then he has exceeded the bounds of *his* potentialities. He can undoubtedly ascertain the *conviction* of many people in the early church that Jesus had risen. But in doing this he has not discovered anything about the event itself. He must however admit that there are, or have been, many things (events, or 'facts' belonging to the past) which really happened for which we either have no sources at all or (as in our present case) sources full of obscurities. To maintain that the only things which happened are the ones which can be thoroughly documented without possibility of doubt is simply inadmissible. The historian's answer to the question whether Jesus rose from the dead must therefore be: 'I do not know; I am no longer able to discover.' But then this answer must suffice the Christian too, in so far as he is concerned to establish the resurrection as event. If he uses his belief (or his spiritual knowledge) to maintain the factual nature of Jesus' resurrection he is exceeding the bounds of *his* potentialities and is speaking without due consideration.

Now I said that the believer is capable of a particular kind of cognition. He really does 'see' more than other people. But he does not see anything different. The two things must be distinguished. One could not, for example, directly infer from Jesus' words and deeds that these were miracles. The man who heard what Jesus said and saw what Jesus did could simply take note of words and deeds alike. There was no difference between what happened for the people who came to believe in him and for those who (on the basis of the very same words and deeds) rejected or even persecuted Jesus. But the people who believed 'saw' that here God was at work (or so the New Testament witnesses say). We cannot today establish 'objectively' that a sermon to which we have listened was the word of God. For one hearer it is merely an extremely boring discourse. For another the same words are a saving event. 'Spiritual knowledge', however, presupposes the *presence* of what is known. Something is seen behind the event; and this is the something 'more'. But it is not a part of what can be historically established. That is the same for everybody. For this reason one cannot through faith establish events in the past which are inaccessible to historical enquiry. Faith must not be introduced into the matter in this way in order to 'save' the resurrection of Jesus as a factual event.

This attempt has been made in a different way quite recently. On Reformation Day 1967 the leaders of the Evangelical church in Westphalia issued a pamphlet for the churches in which they tried to give advice in the present uncertainty (cf. the Preface to the present book). I shall quote in abridged form and only those passages which touch on our present problem:

'Theology has correctly pointed out that the resurrection of Jesus Christ cannot be proved by the methods of historical scholarship. But if from this the inference is drawn that the resurrection of Jesus Christ is neither a historical event nor a fact of redemption . . . then it must be stated that this doctrine cannot be brought into accordance with the testimony to the resurrection of the Holy Scriptures.'

We could immediately point to the contradiction inherent in these two sentences. How can an event be called *historical* if it cannot be established by historical methods? But I do not want to enter into polemics; my only concern is to clarify the problem.

No doubt the wording has simply been insufficiently considered. What the writers apparently mean is that the factual character of the resurrection of Jesus must be preserved even though the event cannot be arrived at by the methods of historical research. Then of course it must be asked: how can it be maintained that an event has happened if historical research cannot do so? And then we should have to repeat what we have already said. But here the problem is really rather different. The answer we are given here to the question of how we know that the event really took place is not 'through faith, through spiritual knowledge'; it is 'from the Scriptures'. Up to a point we must agree that this answer is correct. But does it really take us any further?

As our lectures have already shown, there is no doubt that the authors of the New Testament writings (or, to be accurate, the authors of some of them) were convinced that the resurrection of Jesus actually took place on the third day after the crucifixion. Anyone who says that this was not a real event is therefore saying something different from what these writers thought. But is he therefore necessarily wrong? It must at least be admitted that the authors of the texts were expressing *their* view, while the person who says something different is expressing *his*. The two opinions may diverge. But then it must surely be permissible to discuss the question of who is right. For if one is dealing with an event, one is dealing with something which is within the competence of the historian. One cannot discuss faith; one can only confess it. But historical judgments are in principle open to examination, although whether this examination will produce results is another matter. The authors of these (few) New Testament writings are communicating their view of the event (of which they were not, after all, themselves witnesses) and this view embodies a historical judgment which, basically speaking, cannot elude the attempt, at least, at an examination.

This is probably the decisive point. In the sentence I have quoted, the phrase used is not 'certain New Testament writers', not even 'the New Testament'; it is not the view of the *writers* nor *their* historical judgment; the phrase used is 'the Holy Scriptures'. And this is certainly not by chance. But at this point the problem of faith enters the field. This sentence takes as its starting point *faith in the Scriptures* – i.e., a contemporary belief. But this point is not brought out clearly. This can be seen if one enquires more exactly into the object towards which this faith is directed.

Let us make the problem clear to ourselves by a process of reconstruction. We will suppose that the women have found Jesus' tomb empty. This was a fact which they could establish for themselves – there was no need for belief here. They now communicate their discovery. Belief is now asked of their hearers, though not (as is sometimes loosely said) belief in the empty tomb; the belief demanded is belief in the women – belief that they are giving a reliable historical report. Now we have no direct testimony on the part of the women, saying 'We found the tomb empty'. The chain of tradition is longer than that. Speaking of belief implies confidence that the tradition has passed on the historical fact accurately and in unaltered form. But how can such a belief be substantiated?

In examining the Easter tradition in the Gospels we have already seen that historical accuracy was treated with sovereign carelessness. No belief can confute this result. It can be disputed on historical grounds. But this would entail using the methods of historical scholarship. These methods, however, cannot prove Jesus' resurrection, as even the first sentence of the declaration we have quoted pointed out. So this road is a dead end as well.

What, then, is the appropriate part for faith to play if we want to make progress? For I maintained that this was possible. I think that progress can be achieved if faith is understood historically but if one does not introduce one's own faith too precipitately. The point at issue is the belief of a third party – the primitive church. Now no one is of course in a position to test the faith of anyone else. This is impossible historically speaking as well. We can never ascertain whether someone else really believes, not even when he says that he does. But it is perfectly possible to recognize the *expressions* of faith made by someone else, if testimony to these exists, as is the case here. We must therefore ask how the faith of the primitive church is expressed, remembering at the same time that the word faith need not necessarily be used at all. We must only see that here a bond is being described which corresponds to what we normally call faith. How is this bond formulated?

At this point the distinction between the subjective and the objective vision hypotheses (a distinction which is in fact useless) can at least perform a heuristic service. For faith plays a different part in each case. In the subjective vision hypothesis it precedes the vision; in the objective vision hypothesis, vision precedes faith. The question is now, what is the actual relationship of faith and vision?

Admittedly we have already seen that we cannot ask directly what the relationship was in Peter's case. This cannot be established, since the assertion that Peter saw Jesus has only come down to us as the assertion of tradition, i.e., as the assertion of others. So we have to formulate the question as follows: in asserting that Peter saw Jesus after Good Friday, how does one represent the relationship of faith and vision?

One does not do this explicitly at all. But the answer is fairly clear none the less, as we showed earlier. The intention is to say that Peter believed because he saw. In what was later asserted, therefore, seeing has priority over belief. But the people who said this had no access to what Peter saw, although they did have access to his faith, or, more precisely, to the expressions of his faith. So we shall have to enquire into these.

The fact that we have now introduced faith into the picture helps us in another respect as well. We have to ask why the statement that the Lord was risen and had appeared to Peter was actually made. The point was surely not simply to tell other people about a marvellous experience which Peter had had – although this motive undoubtedly played a part. But the purpose was *also* to call others to the same faith which had been seen in Peter and which the speaker now shared with him. This statement is therefore both a testimony to the faith of another and a personal profession of faith. Personal faith is confessed and others are called to share in it. Now the whole framework of this statement becomes clear: the starting point is the faith of Peter (faith which is traced back to a vision of Jesus); this faith is shared by the speaker; and it is the starting point from which others are called to the same faith.

But what part does the resurrection play in the statement? Again, instead of asking this directly let us keep to faith. Faith always has an object – it is always faith *in*. Now of course we can swiftly answer that we are speaking of faith in Jesus. This is true enough as far as it stands, but it remains a purely formal statement which really tells us nothing; it is in itself meaningless.

This remark may seem a surprising one. For every Christian will say that his faith in Jesus is anything but meaningless. That is true, but only because, almost without thinking about it, he associates a great deal with his faith: a particular sort of behaviour; a particular kind of attitude; a particular mode of conduct; a particular hope for the future. And the Christian reads all this into the sentence. But is he right to do so?

First one must realize that faith in Jesus is a purely formal phrase which is in itself completely without content. In the same way, when one says that the important thing is to acknowledge Jesus as Lord, this is true; but what does it mean? If one asks someone what it means, one will probably be told that it means serving Jesus, belonging to him, letting him direct one's life, and what one says and does. But this does not take one beyond the formal scaffolding.

Let us take an image still belonging to the world of the New Testament. If someone owned a slave in those days, the master had no importance for the slave as long as he did not demand anything particular from him, thus acquiring a relationship to him. It is only where this relationship is embodied in concrete terms that the master really *becomes* master, although he *is* of course the slave's master even without the realization of this relationship.

The statement that Jesus is Lord says nothing until it explains how this lordship is realized in concrete terms in my own case. If, now, Peter found (renewed) faith in Jesus after Jesus' death, we are bound to ask (if this is not to remain a purely formal statement, and hence a meaningless one) where this faith acquired its content. The usual answer is: from the raising of Jesus. Now we still do not know what the raising of Jesus is. We still do not know how people came to speak of the raising of Jesus at all. But even if we are willing to dispense for the moment with an explanation and simply take the traditional answers, we shall quickly find out that these do not take us any further either. The answer may be that in raising Jesus God acknowledged the one who was crucified; or that God endorsed Jesus in spite of his apparent failure; or something similar. But if we formulate the matter in this way we never say *whom* God endorsed Jesus as being, as *whom* he acknowledged him.

What happened – and now the statements acquire content for the first time – was that God endorsed Jesus *as the person that he was:* during his earthly lifetime Jesus pronounced the forgiveness of sins to men in the name of God. He demanded that they commit their lives entirely to God, that they should really take no thought for the morrow. He demanded of them that they should put themselves entirely at the service of their neighbour. He demanded of them that they risk their lives – and that meant giving up any attempt to assert themselves. He demanded of them that they work for peace even where it was dangerous, humanly speaking, because it could mean relinquishing one's own rights. And he promised people that in fulfilling this demand they would find true life, life with God. I could easily add a whole catalogue of other statements. Where does the substance of these statements come from?

The faith which Peter found after the death of Jesus, which others then came to share and into which they then called yet others, can be defined in substance by saying that it was the faith to which Jesus of Nazareth had called men. It was for this reason that I deliberately called these lectures *The Resurrection of Jesus of Nazareth*. The designation 'of Nazareth' is intended to bring out the fact that faith after Easter (faith in the risen Jesus) was no different in substance from the faith to which Jesus had already called men before Easter.

This brings us to a very interesting parallel; for we have already discovered the same thing in the Gospels as a whole. There the Easter happening is depicted in each case as a sequence of events which varies quite considerably in the details of its order, topography and sometimes *dramatis personae* in the different Gospels. Yet the evangelists were one in what they wanted to say: the same thing that Jesus offered, brought and gave before Good Friday is to be offered, brought and given after it. Let me remind you how that became evident in the various missionary charges, for example. The Easter stories in the Gospels simply must not be isolated from what precedes them. They present a continuous sequence of events in which the identity of the person once there with the person now preached is expressed in a particularly vivid way. That is admittedly a later development; but it is exactly the same in essence as the initial situation. The faith which Peter held after the death of Jesus, a faith into which others were then drawn (and it is only their statements which are available to us) and the faith into which these people called yet others – this faith did not differ in substance from the faith to which Jesus of Nazareth called men.

This is what I meant when I wrote earlier that Easter meant that the cause of Jesus continues; or, in the words of the German hymn, 'Still he comes today' – whereby both elements must be stressed: it is really *he* who comes; and he really comes *today* – and what comes today the same thing that Jesus of Nazareth brought.

How Peter discovered this we can no longer definitely say. Later, people said that Peter discovered it by seeing Jesus. This may be the case. I do not know. But anyone who claims to know better must be able to produce his evidence.

But must not a Christian now ask with fear and anxiety: does this not cast everything into doubt? Has not the ground been cut away from under the feet of our faith? To this I would answer: for my faith in Jesus, it is completely unimportant *how* Peter arrived at his faith in Jesus after Good Friday. It is equally unimportant how the person found faith who then communicated his faith to me, so that I, in my turn, could believe.

The ways in which the individual arrives at faith in Jesus are so manifold that no one would dare to set up a standard to which a man must conform before he can properly achieve faith. The decisive thing is that the *faith* is always the same, even though it may be expressed differently at different times. It is expressed differently today from the way it was expressed a generation ago, and of course differently again from the way in which it was expressed in the first generation. But even if the form it takes varies in the course of history, it remains what it always desires to remain – faith in Jesus. Our faith is only the Christian faith if it is joined with the faith of the first witnesses and with the faith of Peter. In so far Peter is really the rock on which the church is built.

The way in which Peter's faith was sparked off after Good Friday is unimportant. One must not say that everything would be in doubt if one could not know and say exactly how faith was born in Peter. Anyone who maintains this must draw the logical conclusion that Peter achieved a certainty through his mode of finding faith which is denied to us but which we ought in fact to share. But then no faith would really have been demanded of Peter at all, or it was at least easier for him to make the venture of faith because his method of arriving at it was of a special kind, the special thing about it being that it communicated greater certainty.

If one thinks this conclusion through, one quickly discovers how dangerous it is. I am being asked to commit myself to Jesus – usually on the basis of the proclamation. (I have already indicated the substance of this proclamation.) Now, I can either accept faith or reject it. But if I say that I can only accept faith if the way in which Peter found faith is certain and can be vouched for, then I am simply refusing to believe; for I am not really prepared to make the venture. I am asking for signs and wonders, even though the signs and wonders I am demanding belong to the past. And that means saying 'no' to faith.

On the other hand it will always seem a miracle that I should find faith through the preaching of the gospel. Another person hearing the same sermon might not find faith at all. I cannot explain why. Nor can I compel another man to believe, even if I believe myself and tell him about my faith. I can only reckon with the possibility, I can only hope, that a miracle will happen to him. If it does, then I can say that here God was at work. But I am not in a position to describe what has really happened.

I hope that it is now clear why I said earlier that the miracle belongs to today. For *the miracle is the birth of faith*. But since it is a miracle, it eludes my description. And that is the reason why I said about the resurrection that it eludes our grasp. For 'Jesus is risen' simply means: today the crucified Jesus is calling us to believe.

This must of course be explained more clearly. We must note precisely how I have just proceeded. I have paraphrased the miracle of my finding faith with the words 'Jesus is risen'. With this I have used phraseology which has been used before, in connection with the birth of faith on earlier occasions. How did people come to use this phraseology?

I do not think that this is very hard to understand. If (in whatever way) a man came to believe in Jesus after Good Friday, he knew himself to be called to faith by the same Jesus who performed an earthly ministry, who called men to faith, and who died on the cross. But if this Jesus was still *able* to call men to faith (and that he *was* able was clear from the reality of the believer's own faith) then it followed that he was not dead but alive. And that could be expressed by saying: 'He is risen.'

But only the man who stood fast in the reality of his own faith could say this. Hence it is not chance, it is of the essence of the thing, that only those who believed told of seeing Jesus. In the same way it was only those who believed who could confess the resurrection of Jesus – only those who knew that *he* comes *today* because they had experienced it.

If we say that Jesus is risen, we are not therefore making an observation capable of being made apart from our own experience of finding faith. But everyone interprets this experience with the help of a particular idea. We must look at this idea more closely before we can ask once more what is meant by saying: 'Jesus is risen.'

VI The Concept of Resurrection in the History of Religion

We must first of all be clear about something which we generally overlook or perhaps do not know, living as we do within the Christian tradition. If someone says today that there is no resurrection of the dead, the statement is usually understood as meaning that 'death is the finish'. For us, hope of the resurrection and hope of a future life are identical. Consequently we assume that anyone who denies the resurrection must also deny every future hope. But a distinction must be made here, for the hope of the resurrection is only a particular form of the hope of a future life. Let me show briefly what this means for the New Testament period.

The possibility of such a distinction is shown by various anthropologies. If (as happened in the Greek or Hellenistic world) a dualistic anthropology was maintained, that is to say, one which distinguished between soul and body or between the 'I' and the flesh, then the future hope always related exclusively to the soul, which was thought of as being immortal. It related to the 'I', to the self, to the inner nature of man, or however it was described. The dualism of the anthropology is shown by the fact that the 'I' is contrasted with the body. When the earthly being (i.e., the visible person) dies, the soul returns to God, enters on the heavenly journey or goes to the place determined for it. Here too ideas vary. There may be some kind of barrier to the future life. Not every soul goes on the heavenly journey, for certain conditions have to be fulfilled. For example, the soul must have acquired *gnosis*, or knowledge, about the path on which it is to enter. This knowledge is imparted to the soul by a saviour who has descended to earth from heaven. According to other ideas, the precondition was to have taken part in the mysteries, in which, through cultic observances, the votary was initiated into the divine way. The god dies and comes to life again. Through the cult it was possible to die with the god and for the soul to come to life again. There were also sacraments. Through baptism and sacred meals the votary was enabled to partake of the godhead, the food being described as the means of immortality. The souls of those who partook of this food were thus secure of a future life.

In spite of the different views about the way in which salvation is conferred, there are certain ideas which are common to dualistic anthropologies. The flesh (or, more precisely, the body) is matter and remains on earth after death; it decays. But that is not a matter for regret. On the contrary, it is welcomed. For this dualism is a cause of suffering to man. The body is the prison of the soul. In death the soul is finally freed from this prison and thus removed from earthly conditions.

To preach the hope of the resurrection of the body to someone who holds this anthropology is not to give him hope at all; on the contrary, one is destroying the hope that he has. For he is hoping to be freed from the body. So nothing worse can happen to him than to be presented with the prospect of the resurrection. If, for example, there were people in Corinth who denied the resurrection of the dead (I Cor. 15.12), we must not conclude that they therefore denied all hope of a future life (as Paul probably assumed, cf. I Cor. 15.32). In the context of the ideas we are considering, hope of a resurrection would in fact rather mean the destruction of hope in a future life, strange though this may seem to us, with our traditional ideas.

In the Acts of the Apostles we are told that at the end of his address on the Areopagus Paul spoke of the resurrection of Jesus. His hearers' reaction is mockery (17.32). Most of them turn away. Nearly all scholars are agreed that this speech was in fact composed by Luke. But this does not affect the question at issue. What is being brought out is an attitude which was widespread in the Hellenistic world: the resurrection is nonsense. Only we must be aware of the fact that the people who thought this were nevertheless themselves far from being without hope of a future life.

It is essential to be aware of another point as well, something which immediately makes the matter somewhat obscure, terminologically speaking. For the word resurrection can be used in this dualistic anthropology as well; but there it means the 'resurrection' of the soul from the body, the ascent of the soul, so to speak – its journey to heaven. The terminology is complicated even further by the fact that one could say that the resurrection had already taken place, a doctrine which is expressly rejected as false in II Tim. 2.18. What does this doctrine mean? The idea is that the soul had already received gnosis while it was still in the body and was therefore already certain of its future; it *had already* risen.

This then meant that the body no longer had any contact with this risen soul. Generally the result was moral licence; since the soul was already certain of its future, the body could do what it liked. But occasionally the consequence was asceticism, since the risen soul despised the body in which it was still forced to remain temporarily.

It will now be clear that in the framework of a dualistic anthropology we cannot speak of resurrection in the sense in which we usually understand it. Consequently the assertion of a resurrection can be rejected as being ridiculous; and the term is hardly ever used. If it is employed at all, it means something different from what we commonly understand it to mean. Moreover, even then it can be used to mean different things. It can mean the return of the soul to heaven after it has left the body, or it can mean the salvation of the soul which has already taken place. The meaning of the term in any given case must therefore be deduced from the context, since it can bear several interpretations.

Now this dualistic anthropology had to some extent penetrated Judaism as well, particularly in the Diaspora, in the synagogues. At that time there were large numbers of Jews in many of the cities of the Roman empire and in the long run these were unable to escape a process of Hellenization. We have various literary documents belonging to this Hellenistic Judaism which show this clearly. But by the New Testament period the Hellenization process had even spread to Palestine, giving a new colouring to the Jewish heritage and producing a number of hybrid concepts.

The genuine Jewish heritage was very different. It was based on a *monistic* anthropology. But one must be cautious in using this term. It is useful to stress the fact that Jewish anthropology was monistic when one wants to contrast it with the Greek or Hellenistic equivalent. For without this contrast of dualistic and monistic it is easy to misunderstand the paired concepts which mark Jewish anthropology. Jewish anthropology speaks of flesh and blood, and also of soul and body. But here body and soul are not *contrasted* in the sense that the soul is immortal and the body unimportant. The soul (or breath) is what gives life to the body. God breathes into the man of dust and gives him life (Gen. 2.7). For God to withdraw the breath means death (Ps. 104.29). Much is not thought out here, for example when we are told that the voice of Abel's blood cried to heaven (Gen. 4.10). In a dualistic anthropology one would understand this as meaning that the blood has the same function as the soul or the 'I'. But that would be a misunderstanding.

It is impossible to speak of dualism here. But since the *pairing* of the terms also makes it misleading to call this anthropology monistic, it is best to speak of a dichotomic, or twofold, anthropology. The stress then lies on the fact that the parts are *co-ordinate* but not *contrasted*.

It is significant that for long Judaism knew no individual hope of a future life. The idea of life after death did indeed exist. One was gathered, full of years, to one's people or one's fathers (Gen. 35.29; 49.29). The dead then led a shadowy existence in the region of the dead (cf. Matt. 4.16). But a future life was expected for Israel, for the nation as a whole, as part of Yahweh's faithfulness to the covenant. Here there is a curious collective thinking which finds its expression in the names of the tribes, among other things. In Jacob's blessing, individuals, the sons of Jacob, receive the promises which apply to the whole tribe (Gen. 49). The father of the tribe lives on in the tribe. The fact that the nation can simply be called Israel, and the southern kingdom later Judah, makes this thinking clear; it is evident from the very way in which the terms are used.

It was only in the last two centuries of the pre-Christian era that hope of a future life for the individual penetrated Judaism (probably from Parseeism) in the form of hope of the resurrection of the dead. This idea was then developed in many different ways, especially in the late Jewish apocalypses. At the end of time, either all the dead will rise, or only the righteous, or only Israel. The idea of judgment is frequently coupled with this. There is also the notion of a double resurrection, the idea of a kingdom lasting a thousand years at the beginning of which some, and at the end of which all, will rise.

Characteristic of this new development is the expectation that the flesh, or body, will be raised. The shades who have meanwhile remained in the underworld receive new life and men will be once more the same as they were during their lifetimes. At all events, the flesh (always in the sense of the body) here plays the decisive role. This is the case even if the body is not in entirely the same form as before, being now without sickness, infirmity or physical blemish. The future world is an intact world. That is really what Matt. 11.5 is saying: that the blind will see, the lame will walk, lepers will be cleansed, the deaf will hear and the dead will be raised up. This is a gathering up of expectations about the end-time. In claiming that Jesus did all these things the intention is to say that Jesus already brings about what was expected of the end-time.

Now we know that at the time of Jesus there was a dispute about whether there was a resurrection of the dead. The Pharisees said that there was. The Sadducees denied it (Acts 23.8); and they denied it for interesting reasons. They represented a consistent orthodoxy. The doctrine of the resurrection of the dead was not a genuine Jewish teaching found in the Old Testament; it had penetrated Judaism through outside influence. The ancient heritage had been altered by what was then a modern philosophy. The Sadducees pointed out that there was no scriptural authority for the doctrine of the resurrection of the dead. Anyone who was orthodox, who was determined to adhere to 'the faith of our fathers', who did not want to relinquish the Old Testament and desired 'no other gospel' (and this was all true of the Sadducees) was bound to reject this teaching of 'modern theology'. One did not want to fall a victim to 'modernism'! But the Sadducees could not hold back the tide. Expectation of the resurrection of the dead had become general among the Jews. In the second of the 'Eighteen Benedictions' of the Jewish liturgy God is praised as 'Thou that quickenest (or "will resurrect") the dead'.

But this idea soon came under Hellenistic influence also. This is hardly surprising, for it is easy to see how Jews who brought with them a dichotomic anthropology might soon, under Hellenistic Greek influence, interpret this in a dualistic sense. The ground had already been prepared conceptually through the twofold division.

If we now ask in what sense the resurrection of the dead was understood at the time of Jesus, it is hard to find a precise answer, because ideas differed and the concept by itself does not tell one anything about the notions which it embodies. This can be clearly seen in the New Testament. Up to a point we have already noticed it in the course of our examination of the texts. There, resurrection can be understood in highly 'material' terms. This is so in the stories of the empty tomb and in the passages where the risen Jesus can be touched or where he eats with, or in the presence of, his disciples. Jewish ideas undoubtedly play a part here. But running parallel to these are ideas couched in less physical terms. The risen Jesus goes through closed doors; he is taken to be a spirit. This is no longer in accord with Jewish ideas.

A further aspect comes into view when we turn to John's Gospel and look not so much at stories about the resurrection of Jesus as at what is said about the resurrection of the dead. Before the raising of Lazarus Jesus says to Martha: 'Your brother will rise again.' Martha, assuming the Jewish view, replies: 'I know that he will rise again in the resurrection at the last day.' But Jesus now corrects or modifies this opinion by saying: 'I am the resurrection and the life; he who believes in me, though he die, yet shall he live, and whoever lives and believes in me shall never die' (John 11.25f.). Even clearer, perhaps, is another saying of Jesus found in the Fourth Gospel: 'Truly, truly, I say to you, he who hears my word and believes him who sent me, has eternal life; he does not come into judgment, but has passed from death to life' (John 5.24). This could have been said by a Gnostic, for what is being asserted is the very thing that is rejected as false doctrine in II Tim. 2.18: eternal life is *here and now*. He that believes *has* eternal life and will not be judged later. To say that John did not understand this saying in a Gnostic sense is another matter. That must be proved exegetically. In our present context the point is merely to show what widely differing ideas about the resurrection are to be found in the New Testament and what the roots of these ideas are. The way in which the different ideas permeate John's Gospel is especially noticeable – how they run parallel to one another, in some cases standing side by side in a completely unrelated way. The almost Gnostic-sounding sayings we have mentioned can be matched by highly 'physical' Jewish conceptions. Although Lazarus has been four days in the grave (John 11.17) so that his body is already stinking (John 11.39) he comes out of the grave in bodily form.

All this shows that it is impossible to speak of *the* New Testament view of the resurrection of the dead. If there are people (and they do exist) who think that as Christians we are bound to take over the *conceptions* of the New Testament, one must then ask – which conceptions? And since there is a variety to choose from, who is to decide which ones are to be taken over?

But perhaps the New Testament is not concerned to communicate accurate conceptions at all. Perhaps the current concepts of the time (which are, after all, quite independent of the message of the gospel) are simply pressed into service as an aid towards formulating a statement. It would then not be particularly surprising that any given statement should avail itself of those concepts which were familiar and current. And in this case it would not be in such concepts that the specifically Christian element need be sought for. There is, after all, no specifically Christian language;

the preacher simply takes the language that is available. Translation into another language does not mean a change in the message. Why should this be the case when the prevailing concepts change? We must only be sure that the message – formulated in a new language and with the help of other ideas – remains as close as possible to the original.

But this is to anticipate. We must first pick up the threads which we let fall earlier.

VII The Resurrection of Jesus: One Interpretation among Others

I said earlier that the experience of being called to faith by Jesus was interpreted with the help of already existing ideas. Let me show in more detail what I mean. Someone discovers in a miraculous way that Jesus evokes faith even after his death. He now asks what makes it possible for him to find faith in this way. The reason is that the Jesus who died is alive. He did not remain among the dead. But if one wanted to claim that a dead person was alive, then the notion of the resurrection of the dead was ready to hand. So one made use of it. In so doing there was no need to pin oneself down to a particular form of this idea, at least not at the beginning; and it is quite possible that different notions were associated with the doctrine in different sections of the primitive church. But the common formula 'Jesus is risen' could still be used. Or one could even go one stage further in interpretation and say: 'God raised Jesus from the dead.'

It is undeniable, I think, that we are here dealing with an interpretative statement. For no one saw the resurrection of Jesus; at least we know of no one who claimed to do so. But this shows sufficiently clearly how the declaration that Jesus had risen came to be made: it was an inference – an inference derived from personal faith. Even if Peter found faith because he saw Jesus, that would not affect our conclusion that talk of the resurrection of Jesus was reasoning from effects to cause; that is to say, it was an interpretation.

Now my calling Jesus' resurrection an interpretation has roused passionate opposition. In particular, the reproach has been made that if the resurrection is an interpretation we should no longer have to do with a reality.

I shall go into this objection in a moment; but first let me point out the curious method of argument. The proceeding is to work from the conclusion to the consequences which that conclusion must inevitably bring in its train. And since these consequences are considered indisputably wrong, the deduction is that the conclusion must be false as well. This form of reasoning is very popular nowadays; but it must be obvious to everyone that this is no counter-argument at all. If my conclusion is to be proved false, the critic must show where my argument has gone astray. Of course I can have gone wrong at some point. If anyone shows me where, I am naturally perfectly ready to admit the error; or I can try to find better reasons for standing by my opinion. But one cannot confute a conclusion by pointing to its possible consequences.

Let me now look at the objection itself. The objection to my designation of Jesus' resurrection as an interpretation is that the resurrection then ceases to be a reality and that Jesus is in this case not truly risen. But if Jesus is not truly risen we can no longer confess today that he is. If we still want to confess that Jesus is risen we must, we are told, cling to the reality of the resurrection as a factual event.

Let us examine these objections. They move in the same circle that we have already come across several times. The resurrection as a factual event in the past is the precondition for a confession of faith in the resurrection today. Our confession of faith in the resurrection today is not the expression of a reality unless it can appeal to a reality in the past. Let us break into this circle and separate past from present for a moment.

It is important to recognize that the early church was undoubtedly interpreting a reality, the reality of personal faith. This reality was felt to be a miracle: here God was at work. In order, now, to express this divine activity – in order to hold fast to God's pre-eminent part in the birth of one's personal faith – it was interpreted with the help of the statement: Jesus is risen.

We must see exactly where the miracle lies. For the miracle is not the resurrection of Jesus, as one all too easily says; the miracle is the finding of faith. The early church was anxious to express this arrival at faith *as a miracle*. It is a miracle, something with which no one could reckon, because Jesus had, after all, died; and this miraculous character was expressed *by means of* the declaration: Jesus is risen.

Now one must not detach the interpretation (Jesus is risen) from what is being interpreted (the finding of faith) and *then* say that the interpretation has independent reality – that it has reality apart from the reality which one has experienced. The texts themselves make it clear that this is inadmissible. It is only those who believed, we are told, who saw Jesus. It is impossible to detach the vision from the reality of faith – and in the same way it is only those who believe who confess that Jesus is risen. A man who wanted to talk of the resurrection of Jesus apart from his own arrival at faith would be bound to talk about it without believing in it. And that is impossible. He would then also have to commit himself to one of the various concepts of the resurrection. With this he would be making the resurrection a verifiable event.

In the early church, therefore, the reality lay in the having found faith and it is the miraculous character of *this* reality which is denoted by the phrase 'Jesus is risen'. One must be clear about the fact that isolated talk about the reality of Jesus' resurrection would no longer be talk about a miracle at all. It would simply be the report of a somewhat unusual event. And this event would *have* to be open to historical research.

We must be very careful about our definition of a miracle. Things are always happening which one cannot explain, but one must not therefore immediately call them miracles. Theologically speaking, one can only talk of a miracle if one is claiming divine intervention. But it is important to note that the *visible* result of this intervention (healing, exorcism, the raising of the dead) is not visibly *miraculous*. The visible fact can be tested; it can be tested even if it is not precisely an everyday phenomenon and even if its occurrence cannot be explained. The fact itself is visible to all. If there are witnesses to a fact in the past, the historian can make contact with the fact later. But he could never proclaim it to be a miracle. Only the person who experienced the fact can do that. For if, in the face of a verifiable reality, someone acknowledges that here God intervened, he is interpreting an established reality as a miracle. The miracle can then be called the reality which God has brought about; but it can only be called this in association with *the thing which* God brought about. And *that* is visible to all.

Now, in our historical enquiry into the background of our texts, we do not come upon the fact of Jesus' resurrection; we come upon the faith of the primitive church after Jesus' death. This belief, or the expression of it, is a verifiable reality. At the same time we find the assertion that this reality had come into being through a miracle. And the miraculous nature of this reality was expressed through the concept of the resurrection. When I therefore say that talk of the resurrection of Jesus is an interpretation, this is not to deny its reality. It only means defining precisely where the reality lies.

The same thing is true today. If I experience my finding of faith as a miracle and if I express this miraculous character by saying that 'Jesus is risen', I cannot by so doing say any more than the early church said when it used the phrase. It is a legitimate question, however, whether one is therefore *bound* to express what one means in this way. In view of the confusion about language today, one might even go so far as to ask whether one *ought* now to express it in this way; because to do so is to run the risk of being immediately misunderstood. For that reason I have suggested another formulation – the cause of Jesus continues; or in the words of the hymn: 'Still he comes today.'

Is this to abandon the reality? Only the person who again isolates that reality and looks for it in the wrong place could say so. What I am interpreting is the reality of my having found faith. The reality is not isolated in the interpretation. The interpretation (however I may formulate it) expresses the miraculous character of the reality; it stresses the pre-eminent part played by God or Jesus in the birth of my faith. I cannot impose conditions on this reality of my coming to believe. I experience the reality; I cannot make it dependent on a demand for reality in the interpretation itself, apart from the faith experienced. Then it would again be possible to speak of the reality of Jesus' resurrection without believing. It would then be possible to say 'Jesus is risen' and yet be without faith.

Let us see what this means in terms of preaching. No one would claim that the resurrection of Jesus must be expressly mentioned in every sermon, on the grounds that otherwise it would not be the Christian proclamation at all. Let us suppose that in a sermon the listener encounters Jesus' offer to accept God as Father, to go with him through life, freed from the sins of the past, freed too from the powers which beset us in this world; the listener is then being asked whether he will take up the offer or not. Humanly speaking acceptance is a risk – the risk, for the man who ventures, of entering on the path which can end in the cross. No one can say in advance whether this will be so. That this path is, for all that, the path of salvation is only discovered in the course of the journey, not before. Only the man who takes the risk can make that discovery.

If, now, someone does take this risk and then asks the preacher to whom he actually committed himself when he made his venture, the preacher will say (and will certainly have already done so in his sermon): to Jesus. This means, however, that Jesus is present in the word of the proclamation. The preacher could not prove or demonstrate the fact of Jesus' presence in his sermon. But the fact that he *was* present in that sermon can be experienced subsequently by the hearer who ventures upon the path to which Jesus calls him. He learns, that is to say, that his path (and that path is his faith) has a source. Paul says: 'Faith comes from what is heard' (Rom. 10.17).

In all this the resurrection need not be expressly mentioned at all. But the man who ventures upon the path is *bound* to acknowledge that Jesus lives. For he has experienced the reality of being called to faith by *him*. And no believer will deny that this faith is a reality.

But am I now to try to make the reality of faith doubly sure? Am I even to call in question the possibility of this reality as I have experienced it by making it dependent on some other, allegedly required reality, which is quite irrespective of my faith? That would again mean denial of faith as a venture. The person, therefore, who is shocked when I say that talk of the resurrection of Jesus is an interpretation designed to express the fact that my faith has a source and that source is Jesus – this person can really only be shocked because he is now required *really* to make the venture of faith; he can only be shocked because he suddenly discovers that up to now he has not really ventured at all, that up to now he has not – *believed!*

A theology which makes the possibility of contemporary faith dependent on the 'reality' of the interpretation can only be called a theology of fear. I do not hold out much hope for it; nor could I advise anyone to commit himself to such a theology. Real faith casts fear aside and overrides this bad theology – although I do not say that this is easy, and every Christian knows that there are many failures along the way.

Let us consider another aspect of this whole complex, however. Why is the demand made in certain quarters today that we ought to be able to say that Jesus is risen apart from our own faith? There is, in fact, a legitimate reason for this. The point is to avoid at all costs the misunderstanding that faith *brings about* the resurrection of Jesus. To put it in theological language, the *extra nos*, the 'outside ourselves', of faith must be safeguarded. It is therefore a just concern which lies behind the objection. But it is wrongly pursued if the *extra nos* is divorced from the *pro nobis*, the 'for us'. For the *extra nos* can only be asserted at all in association with the *pro nobis*. Only the man who believes can say that God has called him to faith, i.e., can assert the foregoing divine action. Anyone who attempts to state the *extra nos*, i.e., God's foregoing action, apart from faith, anyone who demands that this statement must be possible apart from faith, is making the *extra nos* a verifiable fact. And the acknowledgment of the *extra nos* then ceases to be a confession of faith at all and becomes a report.

If we look a little more deeply into the matter, I think that we can discover what lies at the root of it. For the demand is not only that we should hold fast to the reality of the statement that Jesus

is risen apart from our own faith; it seems as if the demand can
be met and as if many people are convinced by it. This is because
they fail to grasp one thing. The confession of faith which acknowledges a reality uses a pre-existing concept in its formulation. And
this brings us to the decisive point. The meaning of this concept
is evident. But because it is evident it can be surveyed *even if the
concept is not believed.* And now the *extra nos* suddenly becomes
something which can apparently be stated independently of the
pro nobis because, starting from the *pro nobis*, the *extra nos* is interpreted with the help of a concrete idea. In this way it becomes
possible to speak of the resurrection of Jesus without confessing it.
But this is to forget how the assertion of Jesus' resurrection came
to be made.

Another very important thing has been overlooked as well,
namely that the concept of the resurrection of Jesus is only one
possible way of expressing the reality of having found faith. If
I have tried to do this with the help of the statement that the
cause of Jesus continues or that 'He comes today', there is nothing
particularly modern about this method. We already find something
very similar in the New Testament. The confession of faith in
the reality of the *extra nos* of faith is made through other concepts
as well; yet the reality meant is no different. Let me give some
examples.

In the Epistle to the Hebrews, which expounds a highly original
and independent theology, the resurrection of Jesus is never specifically mentioned at all. Instead we are told that Christ has entered
into heaven and now appears in the presence of God on our behalf
(9.24). We are told that he has passed through the heavens (4.14)
and that he has sat down at the right hand of the majesty on high
(1.3; 8.1; 10.12f.). The literary form of this 'letter' is actually that
of the homily or sermon, an epistolary ending having merely been
appended to it in the last verses. This closing passage does at least
contain an allusion to the resurrection: 'Now may the God of peace
who brought again from the dead our Lord Jesus, the great shep-
herd of the sheep, by the blood of the eternal covenant, equip you
with everything good' (13.20f.). But even here it is not really the

concept of the resurrection which is being used. In the Epistle to the Hebrews we really have to do with the idea of exaltation. The one who was crucified has been exalted; and because he has been exalted he is of immediate concern to the church.

We are inclined to link these two ideas together by saying that exaltation of course presupposes the resurrection. But that is an inadmissible harmonization of two different ideas which we arrive at primarily because we always immediately think of the Gospel of Luke and the Acts of the Apostles. But in these there is a secondary association to which I shall return later. Originally the two concepts of exaltation and resurrection occur separately and parallel to one another.

In the idea of exaltation there is at first no reflection about the mode of the raising of the one who was crucified. The believer only knows – because he has experienced the fact – that Jesus lives. This 'he lives' is externalized with the help of the idea 'he is exalted'; 'he sits at the right hand of God'.

Now it can be shown that the idea of the exaltation is by no means a late interpretation (the Epistle to the Hebrews was written about 97); it can be shown to have existed before Paul. In his hymn to Christ (Phil. 2.5-11), Paul repeats, and in part expands, a pre-Pauline hymn. Its subject is the Son of God, who emptied himself, taking the form of a servant, and humbled himself, obedient unto death (Paul adds, even death on a cross). The passage then goes on: 'Therefore God has highly exalted him and bestowed on him the name which is above every name, that *at the name of Jesus* every knee should bow, in heaven and on earth and under the earth, and every tongue confess that Jesus Christ is Lord, to the glory of God the Father' (2.9-11). It is significant that the resurrection is not mentioned in the framework of this concept of exaltation. Exaltation follows humiliation because of Jesus' obedience. That is the reason why Jesus has a name above every name, that at the name of Jesus – that is to say, at the name of him who was obedient – every knee should bow.

We must notice here exactly what comes first and what second. As the hymn describes it, Jesus has received the name that is above every name through his exaltation. But of course there are no witnesses to Jesus' exaltation, to his sitting at the right hand of God. The statement came into being because it had already been learnt by experience that Jesus has the name that is above every name. What the believer experienced in the faith to which he knew himself to be called is expressed as a miracle through an interpretation: Jesus has been exalted.

One is inevitably reminded here of the close of Matthew's Gospel: 'All authority in heaven and on earth has been given to me.' This suggests the question of whether it is ultimately not the idea of resurrection but the idea of exaltation which lies behind the end of Matthew. We would then only discover the idea of the resurrection in it because of the earlier story of the empty tomb. But the two do not originally belong together. I pointed out earlier that the evangelists forged a sequence of events out of traditions which were originally individual units. If we take this into account we are faced with the basic question of whether the references to people seeing Jesus and the circumstantial accounts we are given of these 'visions' originally presuppose the resurrection at all.

The concept of Jesus' exaltation can be found still more frequently in the New Testament, however. Let me mention two other references to it. Another hymn, similar to that in Phil. 2 though much shorter, is quoted in I Tim. 3.16. Here two ideas are in opposition: manifested in the flesh – taken up in glory. Again, the resurrection is not mentioned – in this hymn not even the cross.

The Gospel of John is even more interesting in this connection. It is true that it closes with the idea of the resurrection; but in the whole of the first part of the work, whenever the focus is on the end of Jesus' life, it is not the resurrection which is mentioned but Jesus' ascent to the Father. 'I shall be with you a little longer, and then I go to him who sent me' (7.33). There are many statements of this kind in the Gospel of John, which could of course be interpreted in the sense that Jesus ascends to the Father *after* his resurrection. But it is just this which the Gospel of John does not describe at the end. Then it is worth noting that in the first part of the work the cross itself is understood as being already an exaltation: 'I, when I am lifted up from the earth, will draw all men to myself' (12.32). And this is interpreted in the next verse as meaning that Jesus says this in order to show what death he was to die. Jesus' crucifixion is therefore already his exaltation.

Now the Gospel of John is of course an example of the way in which the two concepts (exaltation from the cross and the resurrection) later coalesce. It remains clear enough, however, that at an earlier state the two were parallel but unrelated. And the same may be said of the notions of Jesus' passing through the heavens, his sitting at the right hand of God, etc. That these should later coalesce seems almost self-evident but – as one can easily see – this is not without its problems. For originally all these ideas express the same thing. Let me put it more precisely: the acknowledgment of the reality of the *extra nos* of a personally experienced faith is the constant; the concept which this confession of faith makes use of is, however, variable.

If the idea of the resurrection eventually won the ascendancy, towing the other ideas in its wake, it must not be forgotten that this was a later development. For if one overlooks this one ceases to notice that at an earlier stage the ideas were interchangeable. Once we recognize that originally the ideas familiar at any given time were used to express one and the same reality, it should be clear that we not only have the right but even the duty (if we want to be comprehensible *today*) to make this reality comprehensible – which means expressing it anew in *our* concepts.

Since the subject is always the faith brought by the earthly Jesus, Jesus alone is the one indispensable factor. Jesus is dead. But *his* offer has not thereby lost its validity. That fact was experienced at the time and it can equally well be experienced today. Because the subject is *his* offer, I have tried to formulate this reality in the phrase 'still he comes today'. Here the accent is on the fact that Jesus is indispensable, and *he* is present today in his offer. My other formulation is directed more to the content of the offer, part of which I have instanced: the reliance on God in this life; freedom to love; losing ourselves for the sake of our neighbour and the discovery of that as salvation, etc. I have summed all this up in the phrase 'the cause of Jesus'. This was his concern.

I am not trying to replace earlier interpretations of the reality by this one; nor would I maintain that this is the definitive expression of the reality of having found faith. These are simply ways of interpreting the same reality today. It is not only possible but also obligatory to strive for new interpretations.

At least 'Jesus is risen' is not the only interpretative statement possible. It is not that today; moreover (and this is what I primarily wanted to show) it never has been, not even at the very beginning. The fact that in the course of later developments confession in the form of the acknowledgment of the risen Lord acquired a central significance cannot be called mere chance; for the associated idea is particularly close to the statement that the one who was crucified *is alive*. I am even of the opinion that we cannot totally dispense with this confession of faith, at least in our tradition. But we must know what we are confessing through this statement and what we are not. By it we acknowledge that in finding faith we have experienced Jesus as living and acting; we acknowledge the presence of Jesus' past – which is all that is meant by the acknowledgment of the Holy Spirit. But we are not acknowledging any one of the concepts apart from this confession of faith; for it is only within a confession of faith that it is possible to speak meaningfully, theologically, of the resurrection of Jesus; just as it is only by the Holy Spirit that a man can call Jesus Lord (I Cor. 12.3).

VIII Faith as a Venture

Another objection to what is called modern theology is often heard today. People say that here hypotheses are put forward whose uncertainty can be recognized from the fact that other scholars come to different conclusions. And now the churches are being invited to go along with these uncertain hypotheses of a few hypercritical scholars.

The objection is justified in as far as our whole analysis is certainly a hypothesis, although I suggest that I have put it forward with great care and that I have substantiated the various stages of the argument as thoroughly as I could. In this way I have arrived at the conclusion that talk of Jesus' resurrection was an interpretation which came into being in the primitive church. Finally, I have put forward the consequences for our contemporary faith and our contemporary creed. Should we accept these consequences in spite of the admittedly hypothetical character of our historical reconstruction? For I should like to maintain that the consequences are correct even if our historical result is false.

Let me show what I mean. Let me set up a counter-position based on the 'physical' interpretation. Let us suppose that the result of our reconstruction has been the following: Jesus rose bodily from the grave on the third day. This was actually witnessed by certain people – perhaps the guard at the tomb mentioned by Matthew. Jesus then showed himself in his risen form to Peter and afterwards to the eleven (not, probably, to the twelve). They received the missionary charge. Jesus then showed himself to others, ate in the presence of the disciples and allowed himself to be touched. After forty days he was drawn up to heaven in a cloud.

Admittedly we could not call this result biblical or claim that it was arrived at without the help of hypotheses. For it would be necessary to explain with the help of hypotheses, first, where the appearances are to be localized; then, why Jesus is said to have appeared to the twelve, not to the eleven, in the formula transmitted by Paul; thirdly, why the risen Jesus on one occasion shows his hands and his feet and on another his hands and his side; and so on. If, therefore, the 'physical' explanation just outlined were to prove correct, then it too would only have been arrived at with the help of hypotheses. Anyone who disputes this fact either does not take seriously what is in the texts or he has not read them properly. At all events it is a case of one hypothesis against another.

But let us now suppose that mine has proved untenable and that the other is correct. What would this mean for faith?

Let us look at the first-hand witnesses. For them there would have been one considerable difference compared with the time when they had to do with the earthly Jesus. Commitment to the promise of the *earthly* Jesus demanded a trusting faith; and that was a venture. It was impossible to tell by looking at him who the earthly Jesus was. They could only believe that he represented God in this world; and they could only believe that when they acceded to his demand. This commitment to what Jesus demanded had no guarantee behind it. Jesus rejected the demand for signs as a preliminary legitimation. He wanted a daring faith.

A verifiable resurrection, with its multiplicity of proofs, would have altered everything in one respect. Jesus would now have received his legitimation. Who he was would now be a matter of certainty. The demand for signs would, so to speak, have been fulfilled. It would have continued to be hard enough for these witnesses to *live* the later life of faith. But it would no longer have been a venture for the witnesses to *enter* on that life. Indeed it would have been a counsel of wisdom; it would now have been simply stupid not to do what Jesus had demanded. The path of the witnesses would no longer have been the path of faith because Jesus' demand would now be law. The witnesses would have been the only people who no longer needed to make the venture of faith – and who therefore did not need to believe at all.

Now of course this conclusion is no objection to the case we have built up. Why should things not have been like this? But we must then be aware of the fact that more is demanded of us than was demanded of these first witnesses.

What would be the consequence for ourselves? We hear the call to faith. The preacher cannot prove that what he preaches is the word of God. We can only make the venture of committing ourselves to it in exactly the same way as people did in the time of the earthly Jesus. It may be that those first witnesses experienced Jesus' legitimation and then no longer needed to believe. But this is for us completely unimportant, for none of us can experience this particular legitimation. The person, therefore, who believes *merely* on the basis of preaching is really *believing*, because preaching offers no legitimation. If we want such a legitimation today, we shall have to ask ourselves how we can procure it and what the consequence would be if we could do so.

Since (again according to our hypothetical case) we are dealing with the experiences of witnesses, we could only arrive at a legitimation of Jesus by enquiring into the testimony of these witnesses, i.e., through historical-critical investigation. We should have to retrace once more the whole ground we have already covered. Even if, by directing our enquiry differently, we discovered the testimony of first-hand witnesses, we should have to ask ourselves whether we ought to believe *their* assertion that the legitimation of Jesus really took place – whether we ought to believe that *they* were reliable informants.

One might go so far as to believe this; but what would be the result? If we believed the *witnesses* of the event which was Jesus' legitimation, then it would no longer be a venture for us to accept Jesus' challenge; it would then be a counsel of wisdom for us as well. It would be hard enough to put it into practice in our lives; but we should be (merely) stupid if we did not do so. If we believed the witnesses of the event forming Jesus' legitimation, this belief would not be succeeded in our lives by a *second and different* faith (a trusting commitment to Jesus' challenge). Jesus' challenge would then, indeed, still remain a challenge; but only because it is so difficult in this world to practise what he demanded. If we meet the challenge, it is not because we are making a venture but because

Jesus is legitimated and we must therefore fulfil his demand.

It could be that this is the right approach. But then there must be a new definition of Christian faith. The character of venture would then lie solely in our assumption that the witnesses have not deceived us. For this could still be the case; that uncertainty remains. Here, therefore, faith is demanded. But this act of faith once made, the rest of the Christian life would be discipline. Sin would then be lack of discipline. Again – it may be that what it means to be a Christian ought to be defined in these terms. But then one should do so and not leave the consequences of this conception wrapped in a vague obscurity.

If, however, I want to go on calling the Christian *life* faith which must be ventured afresh day by day, then this cannot be faith that the witnesses have not deceived me; it can only be the faith in which I am asked today (and genuinely asked) whether I am prepared to accept Jesus' challenge. This is the point which decides whether I believe or whether I do not. The call to faith would then be the challenge which must be risked. The events following Good Friday (whatever form they took) can detract nothing from this challenge.

But if we insist that the events must be viewed in 'physical' terms of the kind we have outlined if we are to be able to believe – if we insist that faith must be faith in the reliability of the witnesses and that the legitimation of Jesus must be thus secured before we can commit ourselves to him – if we say that true faith is impossible without this legitimation – then we are rejecting faith as a challenge, as a venture. And that means that we are refusing to believe.

Consequently, even a completely different historical conclusion could not be used as a prop to faith if faith is really to remain faith. Here let me stress once more that this (hypothetical) result can also only be arrived at by means of historical-critical investigation. It remains itself a hypothesis and must be called one even if its supporters do not recognize its hypothetical character.

But historical-critical research is not in a position to provide a prop for faith. On that account, however, it is not in a position to endanger faith either. To put it in concrete terms: a 'physical' result cannot offer any support to faith; nor can our result endanger it. But what can it do, then?

Well, it can sweep away false supports and thus show what faith really is. In this way it can serve faith and help it to remain what it really is. Moreover it can show that it is not necessary to take the devious path over these false supports in order to make the venture of faith. Faith itself does not become any easier thereby; but the approach to the decision for faith becomes simpler. These two things must be distinguished.

Modern theology is sometimes reproached with having ceased to make any demands on people. We are told that it seeks to dispense with the stumbling-block of faith and that it takes its bearings from modern man. But this is far from being the case. No theology can make faith any easier. Every individual has to make the venture of faith for himself and no theology can help him. But theology can make the approach to the real questions of faith easier. For who will deny that there are a great many people who, when they hear anything about the Christian faith, immediately think (after the virgin birth) of the resurrection of Jesus, which they can neither cope with nor see beyond? Hence Jesus' invitation to believe never reaches them at all. Again, there are other people who commit themselves to Jesus' offer, but who continue to feel scruples about whether they can properly call themselves Christians because, although they make the venture of love, they cannot come to terms with the resurrection (in the sense in which they conceive it).

If, then, historical-critical research helps to determine the place of the assertion of Jesus' resurrection in the framework of the Christian creed, then it shows by this means that faith in the resurrection of Jesus is not a barrier which has to be overcome first – or even at a later stage. In my view, it is the man who fights for the preservation of this barrier today who is standing in the way of the Chistian faith. The man who feels in need of this barrier, however, should seriously consider whether he does not need it merely because he is unwilling to risk making the venture of faith. And even if *he* needs the barrier, he cannot call other people heretics because they sweep the barrier away, not irresponsibly but for sound reasons.

In this grievous controversy (which affects not only our own church but the Roman Catholic Church as well) would it not be possible for us to agree that the decision as to whether a person is a Christian is made in his life, not in his head? The heretic is the man who does not make Jesus' offer the basis of his life. *This* is the real stumbling-block which we are so ready to evade. And do we not all evade it again and again?

Can a theology be heretical as well? I think that it can. It is certainly heretical if it hinders faith – for example by setting up conditions which have to be fulfilled before one can believe, conditions which therefore create barriers. The task of true theology must rather be to remove barriers, so that people can come face to face as quickly as possible with the decisive Christian question: 'Am I prepared to commit myself to Jesus' offer, which means having to do with God in this world, in this life?' It is this which is theology's task and its ministry.

IX Developments in the Early Church

If it is true that belief in the resurrection of Jesus has in the course of time become a barrier which has first to be overcome before a person finds faith in Jesus, then it would be useful to discover as nearly as possible the precise point at which this happened; we could then avoid mistakes perhaps made in the course of tradition. Let us now look at early developments, not proceeding analytically this time (as we did at the beginning of the lectures) but synthetically. In the course of this survey we shall also make something like a test of our historical-critical enquiry. We saw that talk of the resurrection of Jesus begins to present problems as soon as it is *understood* as a sequence, as a series of events. This does not necessarily have to be the case, however, where the resurrection is *described* as a sequence. One must make that distinction, a distinction which is connected, at least in part, with the fact that we have a different attitude to history from people in the past. But let us approach the problem step by step.

How did the description in the form of a sequence arise? If we leave I Cor. 15 on one side (where we have to do formally speaking only with a sum of several statements introduced by ὤφθη) we are thrown back on the final sections of the Gospels. Our analysis showed us that the evangelists linked up what were originally separate traditions; and, moreover, that they did not take over these traditions unaltered, but modified them so that they fitted not only into their narrative contexts but also into their respective theological conceptions. It is therefore difficult to say definitely what the individual traditions on which the evangelists drew originally looked like. We must put up with this uncertainty. But because of the similarity of certain traditions, a number of things can still be said.

How did the separate traditions arise? In view of some of the things already said, we might be inclined to reply that very early on people detached the concept of the resurrection of Jesus, which was used to express the believer's having found faith, from this reality; and that they went on to develop the concept in isolation. But that would not be an entirely accurate account. It is essential to realize that where we use abstract ideas the ancient world, particularly in the east, frequently used images or picture language. Let me make this clear with a play on words which brings us very close to our particular problem: where we have *insight* into a thing they *saw* a thing. A writer often expresses as a happening a train of thought which we would clothe in abstract terms. What we think of in conjunction often appeared to him as a sequence. At these points we easily go astray in our attempts to understand the ancient account. Part of the reason is that we, living in a world stamped by the Enlightenment, have learnt to distinguish between what really happened and what the thing that happened can tell us, what its consequences are, what it means, and so on. For us the two things are separate; and when we come across such accounts we instinctively make a distinction. Moreover we judge historically. We say that this or that did not happen as people then described it as doing. Our judgment is undoubtedly correct. But we all too easily overlook the fact that it is anachronistic; for we are bringing to the texts a distinction which was still foreign to the authors. It is then easy to say: that did not happen, *therefore* it is not a reality.

But the authors start from a reality. They came to believe in Jesus after Good Friday. They express this in pictorial terms. But what they want to say is simply: 'We have come to believe.' Because they make this reality their starting-point they can externalize it in different ways, without feeling any contradiction thereby. It really is possible to visualize the same reality in different ways. Let me remind you of the parallel ideas of resurrection and exaltation. When we look at these individual traditions, however, we are first struck by the visualizations used and look for historical reality in them. Hence we arrive at the verdict that the stories contradict one another, that they cannot be harmonized and that they therefore cannot be historical.

Now everything really depends on our understanding our different ways of looking at things, on our conscious recognition of what is at the back of our minds when we look at texts of this kind. Only then will this subconscious interpretation avoid becoming a prejudice. If it does become one, we are barring the way to an understanding of the early texts; because we are then presupposing, without further reflection, that the authors of these early texts thought and described events in exactly the same way as we ourselves. The result will be an impossible sentence like the one in the Düsseldorf Declaration – that it is false doctrine to maintain that the Easter witnesses did not intend to report the appearances in the form in which they occurred.

In this connection I should like to say a word about the concept of legend. One often reads or hears it said that the Easter stories in the Gospels are legends. A statement of this kind always immediately rouses fierce opposition. But that is because people are not clear about the nature and definition of a legend – and indeed because the word is not always used in a precise sense. When we talk about the formation of a legend today we usually mean stories which are told about somebody but which did not really take place. We then generally go a step further and conclude that the stories are simply untrue. Historically speaking this judgment may be in a sense correct. But nevertheless, we ought to be cautious even here. For example, a good anecdote about a certain person can describe an incident which, even though it did not take place in this way, is a precise characterization of that person. As a characterization of the person the story is true, even if the facts which are related never happened. The matter only becomes dangerous if one detaches the facts related from the reality which they express (for example a person's loyalty); that is to say, only when one ceases to understand that story in the sense in which it was conceived (namely as the characterization of someone's loyalty). It is only then that to speak of 'the formation of a legend' becomes a derogatory phrase. But it is obvious, I think, that legends ought not to be looked at in this way.

If, now, a person's loyalty is described in two different legends, one must not conclude that this shows that he was loyal twice. Both legends intend to say the same thing. If they are the work of two different writers it follows that both want to express the same loyalty, although they describe it in different ways. If the legends are the work of a single author, his aim is to express that this person was very loyal, that his loyalty was consistent. The number of the legends does not therefore increase the quantity – it underlines the quality; or it may be the expression of a widely accepted conviction of one and the same reality (the loyalty of this particular person).

Now it must always be remembered that to call individual Easter stories legends is not to express a historical judgment about them. The word legend is sometimes applied in this sense, but it is then being misused. To call a story a legend is to express an opinion about its *literary form*. The term legend is somewhat equivocal, but its distinguishing mark is its intention to characterize people. The author's aim is to edify, not inform; he is making an appeal to the reader. This appeal can undoubtedly be made through features which are pure embroidery. The truth of such legends is not determined by whether the event depicted took place as it is described as doing, but by whether the pictorial terms chosen are true to the reality which is to be expressed. Hence legends can contradict each other in their method of narrative or description without necessarily contradicting one another in what they have to tell.

Anyone who does not understand this characteristic will always arrive at a false judgment. But once this peculiarity is recognized, it opens up a suitable approach to an understanding of the different traditions which lie *behind* our Gospels. Let me give one or two examples.

(*a*) The missionary charge (in its varying forms) presupposes the having-found-faith. This in its turn implies the necessity of calling others to the self-same faith. This is presented as Jesus' giving of the missionary charge – perfectly correctly, this being an experienced reality. But the reality can be embodied in varying terms. The wording of the missionary charge, the place where it was given, the accompanying circumstances – none of these are important. Here variations could be introduced, and were introduced, as we have seen. Other statements about Jesus were also made in the same context. For example, we read in Matthew that all authority in heaven and on earth has been given to him. I have already indicated the connection of this statement with the idea of exaltation. Jesus is never described as 'the risen' Lord; and I therefore think it probable that these appearance stories were originally designed to describe appearances of the exalted, not the risen, Jesus. Jesus appears from heaven, so to speak. The impression that he had risen from the grave only arises from the sequential nature of the account in our present Gospels.

(*b*) The same idea (mission) can also be formulated by calling Peter (and then the other disciples) fishers of men. I think that it is highly probable that the oldest externalization of Jesus' commission lies *behind* John 21. If this is correct, then one can certainly draw the historical conclusion that the disciples returned to Galilee after Jesus' crucifixion. There Peter realized – he *saw* – (perhaps while fishing?) that Jesus was sending him forth. This is described with the help of the story of the miraculous draught.

But now something curious happens. This Easter experience is projected back into the lifetime of Jesus, in very brief form in Mark 1.17 and then, with much greater elaboration, in Luke 5.1-11. It must be recognized that this is completely appropriate, even if we come to the conclusion that it is unhistorical. Such a judgment, though historically correct, is entirely irrelevant. The point after Good Friday was the faith in which Jesus of Nazareth established men. The one who calls is the unchangeable one; the Jesus who calls after Good Friday is the Jesus who was there before. The experience of later faith now determines the description of the earthly Jesus. But the reverse is also true: the picture which one has of the earthly Jesus provides the material for an externalization of the having-found-faith after Good Friday. Thus the impression grows that Jesus' life continues for a little longer on earth. The 'earthly' Jesus meets with the disciples after his death, talks to them and sends them forth.

This intermingling of images of the earthly Jesus and images created by later faith in him naturally makes it hard for *us* to arrive at the historical Jesus (in the sense in which we understand the term). But, to revert to our play on words, we must understand that the disciples, having found faith after Good Friday, acquired *insight* as to who Jesus was and now *see* him like this as well. They are therefore depicting a reality, though of course not a historical reality. Anyone who looks for *direct* history in these images has simply failed to grasp their character.

(c) The story of the Emmaus disciples has been expanded by Luke. The conversation on the road bears a typically Lucan colouring, although it is difficult to be certain where the dividing line between tradition and editing is to be drawn. Jesus' manifestation of himself at supper is unmistakably the centre of the story, however. I therefore think it very probable that this story was originally designed to exemplify the presence of Jesus at the common meal of the early church – a presence which had been constantly experienced as reality.

After all we still speak today of the presence of Jesus at the Lord's Supper or the Holy Communion. We formulate this in dogmatic terms. Earlier writers expressed it in pictorial ones. But the same reality is meant. That fits in with the prayer which we know was part of the liturgy of the common meal in the early church – 'Maranatha – come Lord (Jesus)' (I Cor. 16.22; Rev. 22.20). There are frequent exegetical disputes as to whether this is a prayer that the Lord should come in the *parousia* or to the sacred feast. I think that this is a false alternative. It springs from Indo-Germanic temporal *thinking*. For Semitic temporal *experience* it is no alternative at all. The coming Lord, whose coming is expected in the end-time, anticipates this coming at his supper. There the one who is to come is experienced as the one who is present, vanishes from the eyes of his disciples (as in the Emmaus story) – and is once more the one that is to come.

At this point one ought really to enter into a detailed discussion of the sayings about the Son of man. It would then be possible to show, as I think, that in addition to the two ideas of resurrection and exaltation, we have to do here with another, originally independent idea which embodies the having-found-faith. The Jews expected the coming of the Son of man in the Last Days. The church now expected the coming of the Son of man, Jesus. This therefore was the embodiment of faith as hope. This hope, however, again had its basis in the faith in which Jesus established men. Hence the earthly Jesus is described and named (even if indirectly) as the Son of man who has already been present on earth.

(*d*) In contrast to these examples, the stories of the empty tomb form a special case. We have seen that Mark offers the earliest available form of the story. I have already pointed out its curious features. The women do not first discover the empty tomb and then, with the help of the 'interpreting angel', go on to deduce from it Jesus' resurrection. Exactly the reverse is the case. First the young man says: 'You seek Jesus of Nazareth, who was crucified. He has risen, he is not here' – and he then points to the empty tomb. The message of the resurrection, which already exists as a formula, is therefore interpreted in visual terms. This must have taken place in Jewish-Christian circles, for there the concept of resurrection from the grave was a familiar one. When this externalization was carried through – whether it was early on or relatively late – can no longer be said with certainty. At all events it is noticeable that the story is complete in itself. It calls for no sequel describing, for example, the seeing of the risen Jesus. *We* only have this impression because we know the later gospels. At the beginning, however, the fact was that each one of these stories was an expression of one and the same reality: the one who had been crucified did not remain among the dead; he is Lord; he sends out his followers to call others to faith. A real problem only arises because this reality was depicted more than once and because the various externalizations of it came to stand side by side. But even that does not have to be understood as a sequence, for the one reality is being stated in various ways and these supplement one another. One does not necessarily have to understand: (1) the one who was crucified was raised to life again; (2) the living Jesus reveals himself; (3) he is experienced as being present at the breaking of bread; (4) he sends his disciples forth to call others to faith. One might rather put it as follows: the living character of the one who was crucified is experienced in the call to faith, at the breaking of bread, and also in the missionary charge. This would present relatively few problems. That is why I made a distinction earlier, saying that simply *depicting* a sequence was not the same thing as *understanding* the account as a sequence.

Let us now look at the way in which the traditions coalesced. Here we must start from the story of the empty tomb, which is the only Easter story found in Mark. Scholars are agreed that Mark worked from an account of the passion which was itself already a compendium of what were originally separate units of tradition. Mark then expanded this account. One cannot say definitely whether this earliest passion story finished with Jesus' crucifixion or whether it already included stories about the burial and the empty tomb. There was certainly no pointing forward to an appearance in Galilee in Mark's source; that was his own work (16.7).

(*a*) Let us now try to interpret this pre-Marcan tradition. In this connection we must always take one point into account in view of the uncertainty about the precise demarcation line between Mark and his source. The context says that Jesus goes to the cross. But we must notice that neither the passion story nor Mark declares Jesus' *death* on the cross to be a saving event (in the sense of its being atonement for the sins of the world); here it is the *way* of Jesus which is described as a way of suffering which ends on the cross. This way, however, is not a way of failure; it is the way of faith – and hence the way for Christians. Immediately after his first proclamation of his coming passion, Jesus lays down his programme: 'If any man would come after me, let him deny himself and take up his cross and follow me' (Mark 8.34).

This Christian way is, however, the way of faith because Jesus is risen. It is true that it is only right at the end that the resurrection is expressly mentioned, but in fact faith in the risen Lord is inherent in the story from the very beginning. The intention of the pre-Marcan (and Marcan) passion story can be characterized quite accurately in the paradox: the risen Jesus goes to the cross. After

Good Friday the disciples experienced the fact that Jesus is alive; this same experience brought the church to accept Jesus' call to faith and hence also to follow the road that Jesus took; and it now puts its stamp on the account of Jesus' earthly life.

Our Gospels have been called passion narratives with extended introductions, though this is at most only true of Mark. I should like to put it differently: we have before us an Easter narrative with an extended introduction. For it is Easter that determines the account. Admittedly, this must not be understood as if the path of Jesus were a path of glory or as if the passion were only a necessary stage on the way to the resurrection; the glory lies *on the way* to the cross. One does not lose one's life *after* one has tried to save it; on the contrary, the attempt to save one's life is itself the losing of it; and conversely, one does not save one's life *after* one has risked it for Jesus' sake; the risking of one's life is *itself* the saving of it. This is admittedly only evident to faith. But this is the way which faith chooses, knowing that this is the road, not just *to* life but *of* life. We can see how close this is to Pauline theology.

It is important to see that resurrection is not a theme which could be isolated or which ought to be of isolated interest. Faith in the risen Jesus means in Mark arriving at faith *in Jesus*. The content of this faith is explored. It is explored in the passion story with its unfolding of the path of Jesus. If the proclamation that the one who was crucified is risen is the externalized in the reference to the empty tomb and then breaks off, this does not mean that something is missing. The 'sequel', if one may so express it, is found in the fact that (because Jesus is risen) the church is established upon the path of Jesus.

Now Mark goes beyond his source in indicating another 'sequel': the women at the tomb are commissioned to tell the disciples and Peter to go to Galilee, where it is promised that they will see Jesus. Scholars are divided about the terms in which this seeing is conceived and what is meant by it. People frequently assume that Mark is here referring to a vision of Jesus which the disciples had in Galilee, similar to the visions described in the other Gospels. I believe that this is by no means certain, especially since we should then have to ask why Mark did not describe this vision. The Gospel text breaks off at 16.8. It has sometimes been assumed, as I said earlier, that part of the original text has been lost. But is this suggestion not based on analogy with the other Gospels? The strongest argument against this view is that no trace at all of the lost text has been found.

Consequently I think that it is more probable that Mark himself is looking forward to the 'seeing' in Galilee, i.e., he is thinking of seeing Jesus at the *parousia*. The Gospel wants to call people to faith between Good Friday and the *parousia*, and this means calling them to the way of Jesus, calling them to follow him. But following Jesus means taking up his cross. The story of the empty tomb, with Mark's interpolation about the seeing of Jesus which is still to come, then shows where this faith is to be lived out: between cross and *parousia*, for Jesus is risen. I must, however, stress that this interpretation of the 'seeing' in Galilee is disputed. We must be content with a number of question marks here.

(*b*) The matter becomes somewhat plainer with Mark's successors, since we can here distinguish between tradition and editing more clearly than in the earliest Gospel. We know definitely that Matthew and Luke knew Mark's Gospel up to 16.8 and that they used it as a source.

But we must clear up a methodological problem. Our question has a particular tendency. We have a theme which interests us, the theme of our lectures. Now there is no doubt at all that this theme may be found in the Gospels. The question is only whether it can be found *as a theme*. Are the evangelists concerned to tell their readers exactly what happened at the resurrection of Jesus and afterwards? Or are they interested in something else and are they only *using* the resurrection traditions in order to express their real concern with the help of those traditions? They could then undoubtedly even expand, underline and reinforce these traditions; but even so the resurrection of Jesus, not being their main theme, would remain subordinate to *their* concern. Matthew and Luke would no doubt suggest somewhat different answers to this question. If I wanted to go into this in detail I should have to give a detailed commentary on the whole of the two Gospels. Naturally I cannot do that in our context. But I believe that the main lines can be traced even if one does not go into detail.

In general we can start from the proposition that the evangelists presuppose the existence of the church. The church has its problems, worries, needs and questions, which vary in the different environments in which the evangelists are writing. Here they want to help and advise. One could therefore call their writings 'sermons to sustain the church'. In order to carry out their purpose the writers all turn back to the beginning, to the life of Jesus. In so doing they do not simply take over Mark's Gospel; they expand it, comment on it, modify it and remodel it – in part even fundamentally. In the Easter story particularly they expand Mark with the help of other traditions. But this must be seen in the context of the respective works as a whole.

(c) In Matthew's Gospel it is noticeable that, in contrast to Mark, not only is Jesus emphatically presented as a teacher, but also the content of his teaching is concentrated in larger speech blocks: the sermon on the mount (chs. 5-7); the commissioning of the disciples (ch. 10); the parable discourse (ch. 13); rules for the church (ch. 18); the condemnation of the Pharisees, the second coming of Christ and the Last Judgment (chs. 23-25). That Matthew was working according to a deliberate plan is evident from the way in which he finishes the discourses. He always uses an almost identical phrase: 'And when Jesus finished these sayings . . .' The form chosen by Matthew for the missionary charge is characteristic and conforms to these speech blocks. The charge which the eleven receive is that they should make disciples of all nations by baptizing them and teaching them to keep what Jesus commanded. Here we have arrived at one of the evangelist's *themes*. His book, and especially the discourses of Jesus which it contains, has a meaning for the missionary proclamation and of course also for the preaching which sustains the church. Jesus will be with his disciples in this proclamation until the end of the world. What form Jesus' presence will take is not stated. Matthew does not go into what *becomes* of the risen Jesus. He is proclaimed as the present Lord.

But why should the disciples teach people to keep what Jesus, particularly, commanded? In order to answer this question I should have to give a detailed account of Matthew's christology. Let me merely draw your attention to one feature which is, however, characteristic of this evangelist. In his earthly life Jesus proved himself to be the Messiah of Israel. Matthew demonstrates this on the one hand through the genealogical table which begins with Abraham and then falls into several neat divisions: twice seven generations from Abraham to David, twice seven generations from David to the Babylonian exile, twice seven generations from the exile to Christ (1.1-17). These divisions are probably the work of the evangelist himself. If one counts up, one discovers that the last third of the family tree comprises only thirteen generations. This makes what Matthew wants to say all the more pointed: at a precisely predetermined point of time, arrived at by means of certain numerical speculations ($3 \times 2 \times 7$, i.e., after three 'double world weeks'), Christ was born. Matthew's other way of showing this is with the help of quotations from the Old Testament. Again and again the evangelist first describes an incident in the life of Jesus and then adds a stereotyped phrase ('This was to fulfil what was spoken by the prophet . . .') leading into a quotation from the Old Testament. Whether the Old Testament saying was intended as a messianic prophecy or not, Matthew interprets it in this sense, thus proving that Jesus is the Messiah of Israel.

I said that Matthew's theme was that Jesus' followers should make disciples of all nations, by baptizing them and teaching them to observe all that Jesus commanded. It is now possible to put this more precisely, without altering the essence of the theme: they are to teach people to observe all that the Messiah of Israel commanded. Jesus is therefore invested with a particular status. This status is the expression of his authority.

This could be illustrated further from various features, one of them appearing in Matthew's treatment of the Easter traditions. Basically Matthew only offers one thing which is outside his Marcan source: the appearance on the mountain in Galilee with the proclamation of the lordship of Jesus. What exactly his source looked

like is a matter of dispute. I have suggested that the idea of exaltation lies behind it. But Matthew does not consistently abide by the
original form of the tradition. He could hardly do so, since he linked
this story on to his Marcan source with its story of the empty tomb.
It is now the *risen* Jesus who appears. Matthew then joins up the
two traditions (the empty tomb and the appearance on the mountain)
by interpolating the appearance of the risen Jesus to the women at
the tomb – an incident which was probably his own invention.

It is obvious that we have to do here with a presentation of the
Easter stories in succession and therefore with a sequence of events.
Does Matthew now also *understand* them as a sequence?

On the one hand, the answer is undoubtedly yes. This is not
only shown by the introduction of Jesus' appearance to the women
at the tomb; it is shown especially by Matthew's defence of the
empty tomb through his framework story of the guards and the
deception which they subsequently practise. I have already shown
how flimsy this 'framework' story proves to be when it is exposed
to historical examination. We can see here, however, that an
attempt had already been made to counter the assertion of Jesus'
resurrection with the allegation that the body had been stolen.
What defence could be made against this suspicion? The opponents
of Jesus were as unable to 'prove' that the body had been stolen
as was the church to 'prove' that Jesus had risen from the tomb.
We have 'evil tongues' on the one hand and a 'confession of faith'
on the other. But once the confession of faith has been externalized,
such an externalization takes on an independent life; and then
the slander (which is perceived *as being* a slander) can also only
be confuted in visual terms by a descriptive account of the deception.

One might say that this is what happens when one is led into
formulating the wrong question. One must then confute an assertion on the same level as that on which it is made. But this is
the way *we* judge. Matthew had already chosen this level. But
what does he do with it?

It is open to him to go on telling the story of Jesus, right through
the Easter events, as if it were a little piece of earthly history.
But if this is his intention his story has no proper end. To be

consistent Matthew would have had to relate where the risen Jesus was, now that he had risen from the tomb. And knowledge of this does not belong within the framework of Matthew's ideas. But one thing he does know: Jesus is with his own until the end of the world. Thus the *visual* concept suddenly breaks off. But, as if with outstretched arm, Jesus points his disciples forward after his death. Though physically he remains behind he is experienced by his own as the *present* Lord to whom all authority has been given in heaven and on earth. As this Lord he is always with them.

It is important to realize that for Matthew Jesus' resurrection is not a theme in itself. True, where the resurrection is disputed the evangelist is bound to defend it in apologetic terms. But the resurrection itself does not for this reason become for him an object of faith. Matthew may indeed think of the resurrection in physical terms; but the point is not belief in the resurrection of Jesus; the point is belief in Jesus who, out of the midst of death, was given all authority in heaven and on earth.

Thus the death of Jesus marks a caesura. In his earthly life Jesus, Messiah though he was, was still the lowly one. Now the lordship of Jesus is to be proclaimed with all assurance. Consequently the resurrection must be defended where it is in dispute. Even if this defence is couched in the highly physical terms to which the writer was already committed, one must not overlook the *function* of his concept in the framework of the work as a whole. Only then can the concept be assigned to its proper place in the Gospel's total statement. And this statement is: because all authority has been given to the risen Jesus, Jesus' cause continues.

(*d*) Like Matthew, Luke too is concerned to establish continuity with the earthly Jesus. But he works this out quite differently. This is clear even superficially in that he follows up his Gospel with a second work. The Acts of the Apostles is a genuine sequel.

The choice of a substitute for Judas right at the beginning is characteristic. On this occasion Peter says: 'One of the men who have accompanied us during all the time that the Lord Jesus went in and out among us, beginning from the baptism of John until the day when he was taken up from us – one of these men must become with us a witness to his resurrection' (Acts 1.21f.). In the first place, the precondition for becoming the twelfth in the group of the eleven is significant; the candidate must have been a witness to the *whole* ministry of Jesus. Secondly, we must note what this co-opted person was to become: a witness to Jesus' resurrection. This does not mean, however, that the resurrection of Jesus has to be the sole content of the proclamation. The mention of the precondition would then have been pointless. Rather, the content of the proclamation is the story of Jesus from the beginning of his ministry until his ascension.

And yet the resurrection has a particular significance because with that resurrection God has begun the exaltation of Christ, thus guaranteeing through him the leading of the church. And this is of decisive importance for Luke. Whereas during his earthly life Jesus was the only bearer of the Spirit, at Pentecost the Spirit comes upon the church and leads it forward. The assurance that the church has really been led by the Spirit ever since Pentecost, however, is given by the resurrection of Jesus (the resurrection here including the ascension). This is what Luke (who composed all the speeches in the Acts of the Apostles himself) puts into the mouth of Paul at the end of his Areopagus sermon: 'The times of ignorance God overlooked, but now he commands all men everywhere to repent, because he has fixed a day on which he will judge the world in righteousness by a man whom he has appointed, and of this he has given assurance to all men by raising him from the dead' (Acts 17.30f.). The resurrection is thus proof of the lordship of Christ. That is the reason why one must no longer evade the proclamation. That is why the proclamation is a call to repentance; and only the man who repents can endure the coming judgment. Thus the eschatological aspect comes into the picture as well. The proof that God offered through the resurrection of Jesus makes it possible to preach repentance in the name of Jesus, that is, in the name of the one who is now Lord. Thus there is hope for the future.

It is in the framework of this conception that Luke succeeds in adjusting and harmonizing the many individual *motifs* found in the earlier traditions, working them into the story of Jesus. If one sees that, then one understands immediately why it was the Lucan conception which ultimately triumphed in the church. Many a question which may be raised in the other Gospels finds its answer if one turns to Luke: Where is the risen Jesus (the question found in Matthew and John)? How is the story of the empty tomb, with the pointing forward to Galilee, to be interpreted (the question raised by Mark)? In what specific terms are we to conceive the vision which is merely stated as having occurred (as in I Cor. 15)? Luke always has an answer. The result, however, is that down to the present day we all too easily read the Lucan standpoint into these other traditions.

Luke's is a great achievement, but it becomes dangerous if one overlooks the way in which it came about. Material which originally belonged together thematically is unfolded by Luke in the form of a historical narrative. Originally the church knew itself to be endowed with the Spirit from Easter onwards. In Luke this becomes Pentecost onwards. This leads *us* almost inevitably to the question of which is correct.

We can only answer this by noting the angle of approach. If we follow the story of Jesus from the beginning of his ministry through his death, resurrection and ascension and then on into the continuing history of the church – if, that is to say, we read Luke's double work as a history of the church, then we are bound to come to the conclusion that it contains errors and distortions. None the less, in spite of this – historically correct – judgment, the decisive point is that Luke did not, after all, follow the whole story as an eyewitness, writing down what happened at each point. His point of view belongs within the later history of the church. In fact, therefore, he is looking back, even when he is describing a series of events.

The special thing about his situation is now that once having given up the immediate expectation of a *parousia*, people experienced and became conscious of the extension of time. They began to realize that the church would have to reckon with its own history. Luke worked out this experience of time and crystallized it in his version of the story of Jesus. For the questions we are considering (which must, however, be viewed as part of this total framework) one might put it in the following terms: the extension of time experienced 'extends' the resurrection of Jesus. The different aspects of the one Easter message become a sequence and take on independent existence.

Theologically this remains relatively harmless as long as one sees all this in the framework of Luke's *single*, backward-looking conception. It becomes problematic, however, if, as easily happens, one enters into the events which Luke describes. Then, without meaning to, one easily comes to add up the different aspects of the one Easter message and then to think that one can only arrive at the whole through a sum of the parts.

An example will show what I mean. Our church year is due to the influence of Lucan conception. Now, theologically speaking one cannot deal with the church year by proclaiming (in the sermon for instance) *one part* of our salvation at Christmas, a second part on Good Friday, a third part at Easter and the fourth and fifth parts on Ascension Day and Whitsunday. One cannot do this and then say, all these parts added together make up the whole. In fact it is the whole of salvation which has to be preached every time; it is only the aspect which differs.

Luke is simply not a historian of the post-Enlightenment period; he models history from the centre of his faith. In Luke's account too faith is the first thing. When, as a believer belonging to the early church, he looks back, he outlines the ground of his faith as reality in past history. No one is in a position to deny that he believed that it all actually happened in that particular way; but neither is it permissible to detach the reality which he depicts from the reality of his faith. On the other hand it must be stressed that it is only possible to preach repentance in the name of Jesus today because this reality existed. But of course only the person who believes can preach. So one must note that Luke the 'historian' is writing his work from the standpoint of his faith.

If we, however, with the Enlightenment behind us, read his

work in the light of the way in which *we* depict history, the matter becomes difficult; for now all the different aspects separated out by Luke take on *separate* significance. Then we try to read what Luke describes as being the ground of his faith in the past without taking account of the fact that he is depicting the past precisely as the *ground of his faith*.

I need only point briefly to Luke's 'extended' treatment of the resurrection. Even the story of the empty tomb is consistently refashioned. Now it is only after the women have seen the empty tomb that Jesus' resurrection is mentioned. The Emmaus story is prefaced by a conversation on the road in which the risen Jesus instructs the two disciples and with them of course the reader as well (the wording is Luke's own). The missionary charge takes on a characteristically Lucan form: repentance is to be preached in the name of Jesus to all nations, beginning from Jerusalem. After that it is completely consistent that Luke should wonder about the whereabouts of the risen Jesus. The story of the ascension on the one hand brings Jesus' earthly sojourn to a close and on the other forms a transition to Jesus' heavenly abode. Because Luke believes that Jesus is in heaven he tells of the ascension. It is only Luke who knows the ascension story and it is hard to say on what tradition he is drawing. The idea of exaltation is developed; the cloud is perhaps connected with the concept of the Son of man. The separation in time between the ascension and the resurrection, however, is certainly Luke's own work. With the pouring out of the Spirit the real history of the church begins.

Luke was living in this period, and it is from this period that he was looking back. The church has its *basis* in Jesus' resurrection and ascension. But the *content* of its proclamation is the earthly Jesus' words and works. Whoever proclaims Jesus' words and works on the basis of his exaltation (for which God produced the evidence with the raising of Jesus from the dead) is a witness to the resurrection.

We *might* therefore say that it was Luke who in the course of developments set people on the wrong track. But we *ought* only to say this if we intended to judge him by the standards of the post-Enlightenment. And that is what we must not do.

Anyone who reads Luke's double work today as if its author had written it after the Enlightenment – anyone, that is, who reads it as if it were a history of the church as we should write it today – is on the wrong track himself. This can only be avoided if we lay bare the presuppositions of our own questions and the presuppositions of the account into which we are enquiring. Anyone who forces his own questions on the documents will always arrive at false results.

Questioning has therefore become more complicated today. But anyone who goes to the necessary trouble will discover that the thing that we have asked about is in fact quite simple.

X   The Christian Hope

Among Christians and non-Christians alike there is a widespread idea that the essential thing about the Christian faith is belief in the resurrection of the dead. Beyond this resurrection and after the judgment the Christian expects eternal life, which is generally thought of in temporal (which means earthly) terms, that is, as time without end. In German there is sometimes argument about the wording of the Apostles' Creed; the text speaks of the resurrection of the flesh, but some would prefer to speak of the resurrection of the body. [The vagueness of the English word 'body' has spared us the full force of this controversy in England and America. Tr.] This, however, immediately rouses the protest of all those who want to 'hold fast to the Creed', as they express it.

Now it could immediately be asked whether it is right to call belief in the resurrection of the dead and eternal life the main thing about the Christian faith. It is a question not only of the dangers which would arise, but also of the very considerable consequences which have already arisen. The world is depreciated. Being a Christian becomes a matter of the 'spiritual' life. This world is primarily important as a preparation for the next. It is a time of testing in which a man must prove himself. It is easy here to start thinking in terms of rewards and punishments. But where something is done for the sake of the reward, the action itself soon becomes questionable. A lack of consistency appears too. Why do men continue to be afraid of death? Why do they still try to prolong life for as long as possible? Why do they describe this world as a vale of tears and yet fear to leave it? When the resurrection of the dead is set at the centre of the Christian faith in this way, it can result in highly dubious consequences – and has in fact so resulted. This alone would make us wonder whether this can really be the main thing.

But even if we are prepared to move the hope of the resurrection away from the centre, a new problem arises, particularly from the standpoint of our lectures. If the factual character of Jesus' resurrection becomes (literally) questionable, if the factual character of Jesus' resurrection cannot be maintained with the certainty with which it has often been maintained in the past and is still frequently maintained today (in ignorance of the actual problems involved), does this not mean that now it is impossible to speak of expecting the resurrection of the dead at all? The argument always runs as follows: the resurrection of Jesus provides the grounds for the resurrection of the dead. If the basis is now so uncertain, then the consequences will surely be equally so? We shall ask ourselves this question at the end.

Now one thing is quite certain – something to which I drew your attention earlier: the hope of the resurrection of the dead is, at least in origin, not a specifically Christian hope at all. Its roots lie in ancient Persian ideas which came to be admitted into Judaism. Although the resurrection hope was still a matter of dispute in Judaism at the time of Jesus, it soon made its way. The Jews came to be convinced of the future resurrection of the dead and are still convinced of it today, although they deny the resurrection of Jesus (as taking place at that particular time in the past). But even outside the borders of Judaism (in Islam, for instance) hope of the resurrection is to be found. This cannot be called a statement of faith in the real sense of the word; it is really rather a philosophical conviction about what will ultimately take place.

The question then arises, how did this already existing philosophical conviction come to be linked up with the assertions of the Christian faith? According to a frequently heard argument, the idea was 'proved true' by the resurrection of Jesus, since here a resurrection had already taken place. But this argument is a doubtful one in two respects.

The first of these can be seen from our lectures, if what I have said is correct. It is no longer possible to talk so simply of a resurrection having already taken place. This argument would then fall to the ground. Moreover it must be pointed out that the argument is historically false as well. For it was by no means the case that the resurrection of Jesus which was affirmed as taking place in the past soon convinced Christians that now their hope of a future resurrection was finally justified. On the contrary, we must realize that expectation of the resurrection as the expression of *Christian* hope did not exist at first. It only came into being in the course of time.

This is connected with the early church's immediate expectation of the *parousia*. Christians felt sure that Jesus would come again during the lifetime of the first generation – that he would come (according to the concept held) as the risen or exalted Lord, or as the Son of man. That, however, would have meant the end of this world. And where men reckoned with the end of the world in their own lifetime, the question of what would happen to the dead simply did not arise.

Now there had certainly already been deaths in the early church. We know of Stephen's death at least. We have no way of knowing how the church came to terms with it. It may well be (and I think that there is considerable evidence for the supposition) that in the sphere of Jewish Christianity people continued to hold a philosophical conviction about the raising of the dead without further reflection and that no particular problem was felt to arise. Thus the question of the resurrection of the dead was not a question which exercised the minds of the early Palestinian Christians. Perhaps, too, people supposed that the martyr had been carried up into heaven, for according to the account in Acts the dying Stephen sees the heavens opened and the Son of man standing at the right hand of God (Acts 7.55-56). But a real problem only arose where there was no pre-existing concept of the resurrection of the dead, as in Judaism; that is to say, the problem only affected Gentile Christians. Here, however, we are not thrown back on suppositions; we have texts which show us how the problem arose and what attempts were made to solve it.

The earliest of the New Testament writings is the First Epistle to the Thessalonians, which Paul wrote from Corinth round about AD 50 on his second missionary journey, soon after the founding of the church in Thessalonica. Let us take this as our starting point for the moment.

We learn first what the Christian message was which Paul brought to the Thessalonians: the time is at hand; every man must be prepared and make ready for the coming of the Son of God. All who cleave to him he will save from the coming wrath of the Day of Judgment (cf. I Thess. 1.9b-10, where Paul repeats his missionary proclamation).

After the apostle's visit to Thessalonica he had sent Timothy to the church there. Timothy has meanwhile returned, bringing good news, generally speaking. In spite of persecution, the church has kept its faith. At the same time, however, Paul now learns of deaths that have taken place, deaths with which the Thessalonians cannot come to terms: Christians are mourning their dead.

This shows clearly that in his missionary preaching and during his stay in Thessalonica Paul had not spoken of the resurrection hope. Why should he? It was unnecessary in view of the imminent expectation of the second coming of Christ.

But now the time appointed for this second coming begins to present a problem, for the Thessalonians are of the opinion that those who have died in the meantime will have no share in the *parousia* and its accompanying salvation. They believe the dead to be lost. Consequently they themselves are also bound to be afraid of dying before the *parousia*, since they too would then be excluded from the coming salvation. Paul learns all this from Timothy. How does he deal with the problem?

Paul could here have introduced the idea of the resurrection of the dead which belonged to his Jewish inheritance. For he was convinced of it – not as a Christian, but philosophically speaking. He could then have said: 'Why are you worried about your dead? God will not discriminate against them. They will not lose their share in the redemption, for God will raise the dead.'

But if Paul had proceeded in this way what would have been the result? He would not have provided a Christian solution to the problem, for he would not have answered out of his faith but out of his philosophy. Any Jew could have done that just as well.

He did not need to be a Christian for this. Any adherent of a Persian religion could have given the same answer and so could a Mohammedan at the present day. All these would have fallen back on a pre-existing idea in order to clear away an acute difficulty in the church. It is essential, I think, to be clear about this.

If someone today wants to come to terms with the question as to what will happen to him after he is dead, he can of course fall back on the *idea* of the resurrection. But he must be clear about the fact that this would not be a specifically Christian support. Anyone who wants to be helpful as a Christian must begin differently. And this is what Paul does. Let me show this from I Thess. 4.13-5.11. I shall confine myself to the main points.

At the very beginning Paul writes: 'We would not have you ignorant, brethren, concerning those who are asleep, that you may not grieve as others do who have no hope.' The others are the non-Christians. Have they no hope? It is frequently objected at this point that the heathen not only had ideas about a life after death – they had definite expectations of it. People then ask whether Paul did not know this, saying that he is here making too sweeping a judgment. But in this passage Paul is not concerned with possible *ideas* and *expectations* about the future which 'others' undoubtedly could and do have; he is concerned with something different.

The Thessalonians are in danger of falling victims to hopelessness – and thus of becoming like the others. But in what respect are the Christians in Thessalonica different from the others? Through their faith! They believe; the others do not. The reason for their lack of hope is therefore lack of faith. (In 3.10 Paul has already mentioned that he would like to rectify a certain lack of faith among the Thessalonians.) But because the hopelessness of the Thessalonians is really based not on a lack of ideas, nor on a lack of philosophical conviction, but on lack of faith, Paul begins with faith in the very next verse (4.14). For the sake of clarity let me paraphrase what he says:

If you *really* believe that Jesus died and has risen again, that is to say if you *really* believe that God in Jesus has acted decisively on your behalf, then this faith includes the confidence that God will, for Jesus' sake, bring with him those who have fallen asleep.

At this point Paul does not speak of the resurrection of those who have fallen asleep. He uses another idea, the notion of being carried up into heaven. For Paul can change the concepts he uses. Once we have realized this, we understand what it is that he really wants to say: 'If you *really* believe, this faith of yours will include hope.' Where faith is without hope faith is lacking. Hence it is important to believe really radically. The faith of the Thessalonians is in Paul's opinion not radical enough.

The apostle then goes on to stress once more explicitly the immediate expectation of the *parousia*. He speaks of 'we who are alive, who are left until the *parousia*', and stresses that they will have no advantage over those who have fallen asleep. He then uses once again the idea of being taken up into heaven. At the last trump the dead in Christ and 'we who are alive, who are left shall be caught up together . . . to meet the Lord in the air'. He then speaks once, *within* this *same image*, of the raising of the dead.

In Luther's Bible and in certain commentaries this passage is headed 'Of the resurrection of the dead'. This heading is misleading, for the passage is not about the resurrection of the dead at all. That is not Paul's theme. It is only mentioned once in passing, and even then within the framework of another concept. The real subject is: faith includes hope. It is important to recognize this theme first of all.

Then (but only then) it may also be added that there is no doubt at all that Paul was convinced that the resurrection would take place. But it is clear that this is a part of his outlook as a former Pharisee. Nor does Paul proceed to offer the Thessalonians a way out of their perplexity with the help of a philosophy. This would not indeed have been a Christian solution if Paul had offered it. He chooses another way. He falls back on faith. He says that true faith includes hope. This is what makes his remedy 'Christian'. As an illustration of this hope, he naturally makes use of concepts which have been taken over from his earlier life.

But now we must also note the way in which the exposition continues. The question which arose was, what happens to the dead who have died before the *parousia?* Now there is the danger that in gazing fixedly towards the day of the *parousia* the Thessalonians will neglect the present. So Paul tells them that he does not need to say anything about the time appointed for the *parousia.* The Thessalonians know that it will come suddenly. If anyone tells them that there is still time enough, they should not be taken in. But knowledge of the nearness of the *parousia* ought to determine every moment of the present.

The apostle then goes on to develop what believing radically really means. This faith is realized where the Thessalonians already live as children of the coming day in the darkness that still prevails (the night). It is true that they are in fact still living in the night and in darkness, but they no longer *belong* to them. They *are* children of light and children of the day. Therefore they ought not to sleep like the rest, they ought not to allow this world, the world of night, to determine their existence. They ought to keep awake and be sober. And they can do this because God has 'destined' them to obtain the salvation which is to come. Faith therefore means allowing the coming salvation to enter the present. The hopelessness of the 'others' is due to the fact that they are asleep, that they have really become *victims* of the night *in* the night. The believer, however, is awake, and as a child of the coming day brings its light into the night which still prevails.

For this very reason, however, *present* faith has a *future* horizon. Where this future is lived in the present, hope is sown with faith itself.

Paul closes his argument (which, we remember, began with concern for the dead) by telling the Thessalonians that the man who believes in this way – the man who really radically believes – knows that whether we wake or sleep (and in this context that means whether we are still alive at the *parousia* or not) we shall live together with Jesus.

In looking at a text of this kind one can of course 'stay one's eye' on the concepts used and then read the passage as teaching about the future hope. If the passage is wrongly headed, this is almost unavoidable. For in face of the fear of death and the agonizing question 'What will become of me?' a search for sources of information is all too understandable. Some people may even find comfort here, believing that they have now been given the information they want. But what happens to this comfort if one begins to think about it? Can it endure?

We are bound to admit that the philosophical notion of the resurrection was in existence earlier. Even if Paul had used it differently from the way he does, it would remain a pre-existing philosophical idea. The fact that Paul shares this idea does not make it Christian. If it must also be admitted that the notion is a widespread one, this can naturally be dangerous for the person who 'believes' in the idea as a (supposedly) Christian one. For now there is the threat that what is assumed to be the Christian hope will undergo a levelling process within the comparative study of religions. That is the reason why many Christians are afraid of research into comparative religion and therefore, urged on by this fear, simply close their minds to it.

But we must be clear about the fact that this ostrich-like policy, carried out in the face of the indisputably parallel concepts found in other religions, is *also* the fruit of fear. But the person who is afraid has no hope.

Thus, in my opinion, a refusal to take account of the philosophical character of the resurrection hope is fatal in view of what is after all the indisputable reality of our own coming deaths. Here self-deception can have no point. I am bound to admit that my own death, which is a matter of certainty, is too serious for that. I admit quite frankly, therefore, that if I had bound myself to this *idea*, had placed my hope *there*, I would see my hope disappear together with the idea rather than clutch convulsively at it merely for the sake of having hope of some kind. For *this* hope would be self-deception. And hope without foundation is no hope at all. In dispassionate moments I could not avoid admitting this to myself.

But where can we turn then? I think our only help is to be found in sober, down-to-earth reasoning. We must be honest. Let us rather be content to stammer or admit that we do not know, rather than say more than we can justify.

In other words, when we have seen that this idea *is* merely an idea and have honestly admitted that we can no longer share it (I should like to say: when we have admitted that it is impossible to share it today), then we suddenly discover that these were only ideas for Paul too. Then we are free really to hear what the text has to say (without the colouring given by the wrong heading). Then we can begin to ask for the first time what the really important thing for Paul was.

Of course he could not simply cast away all his ideas or his philosophy. Who can? But we can now see, because we have become free to do so, that Paul did not want to communicate ideas but used them as images to express what he thought as a Christian. Paul is not talking about the resurrection of the dead; he is talking about faith. And he says that the person who is afraid (even of death – or especially of death) must cling to faith, must make the venture of a far more radical faith. For only radical faith can lead the way out of fear.

It must not be overlooked that Paul was speaking to living people who were mourning their dead but who were now afraid that they too might die before the *parousia* and thus fail to gain redemption. Fear of death in the future was therefore determining the life of the Thessalonians in the present.

But this is true at all periods. Fear of death is by no means merely a fear of the approaching *hour* of death; it determines in varying form the life a person leads. It shows itself in his urge to assert himself at all costs. It shows itself in his unwillingness to be disturbed, in the demand to be left in peace by other people, by adverse circumstances, or by unforseen events. We are threatened. Fear drives us to the attempt to bring life within our grasp, to make it run according to our plans and to see that nothing interferes. We want to be masters of our lives – and are always and everywhere forced to discover that we are not. We want everything to adapt itself to us. But nothing has any intention of adapting itself to us. Everything that we do is done on the verge of defeat. Can we really live like this? Death does not only stand at the end of life; it accompanies us the whole time, and not only in the simple sense that something can happen to us at any moment (though of course that is true too). The point at issue is something far more elemental: we want to save our lives and can only do so to a very limited extent and for a very limited time.

In this situation we are given the chance of making, after all, the venture of faith. That means, quite simply, not trying to be self-sufficient but letting go. We are offered the chance of seeing through the circumscription of our lives and throwing it aside. We are offered the chance of letting tomorrow's worries belong to tomorrow and not to today. We are offered the chance – a chance which is also a challenge – of seeking out the other person instead of defending ourselves from him.

I do not now need to say who offers us all this. *He* comes today and offers us what I have called the cause of Jesus. At first this offer is simply a challenge.

Then, however (and one can really only put this in terms of a personal confession of faith) I take the risk of doing what he asks, contrary to all human reason. In the course of so doing I experience the fact: it is true. I do not need to save myself, but at the very point where I let myself go I discover that I am being held by something outside myself. Once I wanted to live, but could not do so. Fear stopped me. Now I give up the attempt to live (in the sense in which I have hitherto understood it) and discover that now, suddenly, I am really living. Then I ask myself, how could I ever have called my earlier life really living at all?

I do not want to fall a victim to emotionalism at this point. What I have said is not a description – or an acknowledgment – of a permanent state of mind. For the same thing happens to us that we are told happened to the Emmaus disciples: suddenly he vanished out of their sight. We are back in the old life. Fear is with us again. And we are once more asked whether we are prepared to let go of ourselves or not. Of course it can be a help to remember that this letting go of yourself has already proved to be true life.

But the intellect will not always co-operate. For the realities which surround us are not phantom realities; they have a threatening truth.

But suddenly you take the risk again, contrary to all reason – and then again, and yet again. And one day you discover that you are on the path through *this* life *to* life.

The man who has experienced this can no longer be talked out of it. For he finds (and now it becomes obvious that I am still talking about exactly the same thing through which Paul helped the Thessalonians) that in the midst of night he is a child of the coming day. He learns where he really belongs, even though he has not yet arrived there. He learns the very thing which Paul tells the Thessalonians: faith *which is lived* includes hope, and without hope there is no faith at all.

This is not, as some might think, because Jesus is risen (in the usual sense of the phrase) and my coming resurrection is *hence* assured. It is because Jesus of Nazareth offered this life as a possibility. Jesus is risen in that his offer meets us today and in that, if we accept it, he gives us this new life.

I could equally well put this in this way: Jesus lived and gave a resurrection into new life even before his crucifixion. One could even say that Jesus was risen before he was crucified.

This is what the Gospel of John makes clear in its unique way. Unlike the Synoptic Gospels, John depicts the way of the earthly Jesus as quite unearthly in that he shows him as walking the earth as *Son of God*. This is connected with a particular concept, i.e., pre-existence Christology. The Son of God, the Logos, was present with the Father before his earthly existence. Jesus is always the one whom the Father has sent. This relationship to God does not leave him on earth. That is why John's picture of him is so different from that of the other Gospels. Compare it with Luke's, for example: one could express the difference by saying that in the third Gospel Jesus achieves his being-with-God only through the resurrection, whereas in the Fourth he brings the being-with-God to earth with him.

This is connected with John's transparent use of the word 'life'.

He uses the word to express both the earthly and the heavenly life, whereby it is noteworthy that eternal life is not the after-life but a certain kind of life *in* this earthly life.

Another feature is peculiar to this Gospel. The traditional concept of the expected *parousia* of Jesus is shifted to the present: 'If a man loves me, he will keep my word, and my Father will love him, and we will come to him and make our home with him' (John 14.23). The *parousia* takes place wherever Jesus' word is obeyed, wherever men take up his challenge. It is hence quite consistent when we read: 'And this is eternal life, that they know thee the only true God, and Jesus Christ whom thou hast sent' (John 17.3). Here the future aspect of eternal life threatens to disappear entirely. This statement is so much directed towards the presence of eternal life in faith that the fullness which lived faith confers makes the question of the future uninteresting. John would say that the person who asks about the future is to be pitied, since he evidently does not know the salvation conferred by the doing of the word of Jesus.

It is important to know that the Gospel of John embodies a protest against a one-sided stress on ideas about the future. The expected resurrection of the dead threatened to become of prime importance and the presence of faith in this life was lost. This protest touches nearly on the problems we have been considering. Admittedly it did not hold its ground in the church, where the Gospel of John was subject to an editing process. Distributed throughout the Gospel we find a series of verses containing statements about the future clothed in the old concepts. This is understandable, for John's Gospel now seemed to be one-sided.

In fact, however, this was not the case. The evangelist by no means allowed eternal life to be absorbed by this life. In connection with the raising of Lazarus, for example, Jesus says: 'I am the resurrection and the life; he who believes in me, though he die, yet shall he live, and whoever lives and believes in me shall never die' (John 11.25f.). I think that this is the clearest indication of the real point at issue. The fact of a person's approaching death is not disputed. But death has lost its power because the man who believes *during* this earthly life – and that means the man who performs the word of Jesus – will thereby have eternal life *in* this earthly life; and though he suffers death he will never die, because he already possesses eternal life.

John therefore makes the same statement as Paul in I Thessalonians, but without using the concepts which Paul still employs. We have seen, however, that these were not statements of faith but derive from Paul's philosophy of life.

This brings us to our final question. Can we, or indeed must we, if we today want to repeat the statement that Jesus is risen, only do so in association with certain concepts? We saw earlier that these concepts are indissolubly connected with a particular anthropology. We saw further that the future hope and the resurrection hope are by no means identical, hope of the resurrection being merely one form of the future hope. There can therefore be hope for the future without hope of the resurrection. If we ask how we imagine the future, we must construct an anthropology and can then perhaps, in the framework of this anthropology, outline a picture of the future.

But do we have such an anthropology at our disposal? To say that we must adhere to the biblical one will not do, because it is inconsistent. At least two anthropologies can be distinguished in the New Testament, and even there they cut across one another to some extent: the dualistic anthropology of Gnosis and Hellenism and the dichotomic (sometimes even trichotomic) anthropology of Judaism.

Now the mutual intermingling of anthropologies which already begins in the New Testament influenced later tradition. And this by no means furthered clarification. Let me illustrate this from the third verse of a well-known German hymn, 'Herzlich lieb hab ich dich, O Herr'. The verse runs:

Ach Herr, lass dein lieb Engelein
am letzten Ende die *Seele* mein
in Abrahams Schoss tragen;
den *Leib* in seinem Schlafkämmerlein

gar sanft ohn einge Qual und Pein
ruhn bis zum letzten Tage . . .

One might translate it as follows: 'O Lord, at the moment of death let thy blessed angel carry my *soul* to Abraham's bosom; let my *body* rest quietly without torment in its bedchamber until the final judgment.' The anthropology behind this is clearly dualistic. At death the soul goes to Abraham's bosom and the body is laid in the grave. This anthropology remains dualistic even though we must note that it does at least show some interest in the body, which is not the case in Gnosis. But this prepares for the transition which now leads to the prospect of what is to happen at the Last Judgment:

> Alsdann vom Tod erwecke *mich*,
> dass meine Augen sehen dich
> in aller Freud, O Gottes Sohn,
> mein Heiland und mein Gnadenthron . . .

'Then wake *me* from death, that my eyes may see thee in joy, O Son of God, my saviour and my throne of grace . . .' Who is this 'I' who is to be wakened at the Judgment? Apparently it is the body, for the soul is already in Abraham's bosom. Here, therefore, the background is Jewish anthropology. God wakes *me* (and in a Jewish context that always means 'my body') to new life.

We can hardly echo such anthropological images and ideas. They may perhaps pass without reflection in a hymn. But when one once begins to reflect, one can no longer revert to an existence without reflection. Probably nobody today, if he forms a picture of the future, expects that 'this old sack of maggots', as Luther called his body, will exist again. It decays. But that by no means implies being without hope.

But who am *I*, then? Let me try to formulate it as follows: I am the person who I want to be. That is a part of my freedom. I may be the person who 'succeeds' in life, who wants to be his own master and whose life and mastery will then end with death.

For the lord of *this* life is death. I am therefore the person whose counterpart is death. Since I am afraid of this counterpart, I defend myself against him as effectively and as long as I can.

Or I may be the person who dares to yield up his own life, who dares to love, to serve, to sacrifice himself, and who learns in the process that he then wins life, that he is taken care of. The person who makes the venture, however – the person who tries again and again to make the venture – learns in the process that he is on the way to life through this life, because true life already begins in this world. He does not believe that death is lord. He is the person who then, in faith as he lives it, discovers God as counterpart and learns to know God as one whom he has no need to fear but as one whom he trusts.

I cannot put it better than Heinrich Rendtorff did when he was dying. He asked his wife to listen quietly to what he had to say and went on: 'These last nights I have been thinking over and testing everything that we can know and everything that we have been told about what will happen to us when we die. And now I am certain of one thing: I shall be safe.'

Nobody could call Heinrich Rendtorff a representative of 'modern' theology. But he was a level-headed man who always tried to confine himself to statements which he could justify. The only thing he was sure of on his death-bed was: I shall be safe.

If anyone thinks that this is not enough, my answer would be: there is far more in the words 'I shall be safe' than in all the pictures which one could conjure up. I think that it is right that this should be so. For the believer must not be modest *in his faith*. It is the person who carries over to the next world concepts belonging to this one who is being modest, because he is making the next world conform to this and is thus imposing limits on it.

The believer only radically believes if he believes like Jesus and thinks that, contrary to appearances, God can do *anything*. That is why Jesus makes us free for limitless faith in this world and utter confidence in God for the future. And that is far more than the idea of the resurrection of the dead could ever express.

Index of Biblical References